WE THE CHAMPS

THE TORONTO RAPTORS'
HISTORIC RUN TO THE 2019 NBA TITLE

This book is available in quantity at special discounts for your group or organization. For further information, contact:

Triumph Books LLC
814 North Franklin Street
Chicago, Illinois 60610
Phone: (312) 337-0747
www.triumphbooks.com

Printed in U.S.A.
Trade ISBN: 978-1-62937-668-4

Content packaged by Mojo Media, Inc.
Joe Funk: Editor
Jason Hinman: Creative Director

Front and back cover photos by AP Images

All interior photos by AP Images

CONTENTS

FOREWORD

By Jack Armstrong as told to Alex Wong

This is my 21st year working as a broadcaster for the Raptors, and I've always told people this entire situation was a sleeping giant. Toronto is the third largest market in the NBA and a world class city.

When you go to a Raptors home game, it's a cultural mosaic. The arena is a reflection of the city of Toronto and there's nothing like it in the NBA.

Beyond that, look at the whole experience of thousands of fans gathering at Jurassic Park and viewing parties across the country. The spirit, love, and passion of the fans is everywhere.

After Game 4 of the NBA Finals in Golden State, there was close to a thousand Raptors fans just going bonkers in the lower bowl section. When we travel to play in cities in the United States, there are Raptors fans and Canadian flags at every arena. It is something truly unique and indescribable to the traditional sports fan in a United States market.

Here I am, an American fortunate to be working in Canada and getting to see and experience this and be able to connect with people on a daily basis, having the complete privilege of having to try and explain all of this to my American friends.

Now, I feel like people are seeing this for themselves.

The scenes that come on their television during the NBA Finals were seen not just across Canada, but across the United States and across the world. I've always said if you get some good people to the organization who are committed and know how to run this thing, the sky's the limit. The Raptors hit a home run when they hired Masai Ujiri. He's hit it out of the park. You also have to give so much credit to ownership, management, the coaching staff, and the players. They've all done an amazing job.

For me, a cool moment was sitting on the announcers table right next to the Raptors bench before going on the air to broadcast Game 1 of the NBA Finals. I just sat there for a few minutes to watch the Raptors warm up. When you go through an experience like this, the demands on your time are off the charts, and I just promised I'd give myself two or three minutes to sit there and watch.

The thing that I fixated on was all the fans coming in and getting into their seats and getting ready for an incredible moment in Canadian history of an NBA Finals being hosted in Toronto. The joy, the pride, and the excitement on people's faces, I just looked at that and thought, man, it's been a fun journey and it's all worth it.

The Raptors finally won a championship.

It was well earned and well deserved, and I'm proud to have been a part of the journey. ∎

Kawhi Leonard celebrates as the clock finally runs out and the Toronto Raptors are officially crowned 2019 NBA champions.

INTRODUCTION

By Alex Wong

"BELIEVE IN THIS CITY. BELIEVE IN YOURSELF."

Masai Ujiri, president of the Toronto Raptors and architect of this championship team, uttered those words on media day in September. The franchise was about to embark on the strangest and most exciting year in history. They had traded away DeMar DeRozan, a player who spoke repeatedly about finishing his career in Toronto, for Kawhi Leonard, a stoic superstar reluctant to embrace anything except the task at hand, who was coming off a season in which he played nine games due to injury and demanded a trade out of San Antonio.

Leonard arrived just a year away from free agency. There were early reports he would not report to Toronto at all. Those early concerns were washed away when Leonard did appear wearing a Raptors uniform on media day. Once he arrived, the attention turned to the basketball team. Toronto had made the playoffs for five consecutive seasons, the most successful stretch in franchise history, but they were only remembered by their playoff disappointments.

This season would be different, but under rookie NBA head coach Nick Nurse, the pieces needed to come together. The Raptors started the regular season with a 12-1 record, but the team was still finding themselves as a contender. Treating his health as the top priority, Toronto rested Leonard on back-to-back games and other portions of the busy 82-game schedule. The term load management went mainstream. Leonard played in 60 games. The Raptors won 58 games anyways.

In their preparation for the playoffs, Pascal Siakam emerged into a star, Marc Gasol was acquired at the trade deadline, and Danny Green gave them a championship caliber two-way player. Despite the new additions and development of younger players on the roster, the team still ran through Kyle Lowry, the heart and soul of this team, the point guard who guides everyone on the floor in the right direction at all times.

The opener of the postseason — a home loss to the Orlando Magic — served as a bad omen then, as Lowry went scoreless. The defeat was buoyed by a miscommunication on the final defensive play of the game by Leonard and Gasol, further illustrating the growth required by the Raptors to make the deep postseason run they were hoping for.

Despite their past failures, this Raptors team stopped disappointing their fans in the postseason. Instead, they showed them what the other side looked like. They fought through adversity. They went on the road and followed Leonard — the best player in the entire postseason — to win pivotal games in the opposing team's arena in every single series.

The Raptors won their next four games against the Magic. They went seven games with the Sixers in the second round, escaping by the narrowest of margins with Leonard's series-clinching buzzer-beater in Game 7. Toronto fell behind 2-0 to the Milwaukee Bucks — the East's best team during the regular season — and then improbably came together and won the next four games. In their first NBA Finals appearance, Toronto appeared to be the most experienced team, winning both games at

Pandemonium at Jurassic Park as Raptors fans celebrate the team's first NBA title.

Oracle Arena in Games 3 and 4, and ending Golden State's dynastic five-year NBA Finals run with a Game 6 victory back at Oracle in the last game ever played at the arena.

It was the culmination of a journey many years in the making, 24 years for those who have been following the team since its very beginning. The team that was named after the Jurassic Park movies and wore purple dinosaurs on their uniforms was now standing at the top of the mountain, NBA champions for the first time in franchise history.

What comes next is unclear, from Leonard's free agency and whether this collective group can come together and do it again next season. But for the first time, Raptors fans no longer have to look back or look ahead. In this very moment, they are the NBA champions.

Believe in this city. Believe in yourself. ∎

Raptors 118, Warriors 109
May 30, 2019 • Toronto, Ontario

NORTHERN TOUCH

Raptors Give Warriors Rude Welcoming, Win First Ever Finals Game

By Sean Woodley

Game 1 of the NBA Finals ... in Toronto. What a scene.

Twenty-four years of tension, built up by departed stars and inferiority complexes and a half decade-straight of crushing conclusions to otherwise great seasons, all released in one beautiful, uproarious day. Fans lined up more than 12 hours ahead of the first Finals game in Raptors history just for the chance to watch the game in the famed outdoor haven for priced-out fans, Jurassic Park. Many of those old estranged stars, including Chris Bosh, Tracy McGrady, and Damon Stoudamire were in an attendance, and honoured by the team to boot. Vindication was afoot, everywhere. It was worth every second of the 24 year wait.

Though amidst the excitement and the newness was a touch of realism. Underneath the euphoric haze that hung above Toronto between Game 6 against Milwaukee and the Finals opener, the scent of gravy could be detected. Toronto simply surviving the Eastern Conference blood wars and making the Finals felt like enough to satiate most Raptors fans. Beating the Warriors would have been amazing, sure. It also would have been crazy to outright expect it.

Even without the injured Kevin Durant, sidelined with a calf injury since late in the second round, the Warriors were The Champs. Portland entered the Western Conference Finals feeling themselves after an emotional Game 7 win over Denver. Four games later, they'd been snuffed out by the Warriors machine. Golden State had spent the last five years tossing the good vibes of opponents in the trash.

On Toronto's first offensive possession, Kyle Lowry airmailed a pass to Pascal Siakam in the right corner. Maybe Warriors-induced jitters really were a thing?

As it turned out, Lowry's gaffe would prove to be one of the only bouts of frayed nerves Toronto dealt with all night. With the help of a locked-in supporting cast, the dependability of which had fluctuated over the course of the season, Toronto weathered an 11-point, three-triple first quarter from Steph Curry to escape with a 25-21 lead.

The opening 12 minutes laid bare the all-out approach the Warriors were going to employ to bother Leonard, the MVP of the post-season to date. Toronto's superstar saw multiple bodies at the top of every pick-and-roll he ran. He ran a lot of pick-and-rolls anyway.

"They did a good job in both halves, blitzing my picks and rolls," Leonard detailed after his clean five-assist, two-turnover turn as a playmaker. "Bringing two to the ball, and if I get by that third guy's coming. But my teammates played well tonight. It's a team game, if they (the Warriors) are gonna play like that then guys are gonna play well, get wide open shots."

"Don't try to be a hero out there. Just play basketball. And that's what I do."

Marc Gasol battles for the ball against Golden State's Kevon Looney during the first half of Game 1. Gasol had 20 points and seven rebounds in the win.

Kawhi having his space cramped all night meant the Warriors were always conceding something, somewhere. That something was a line of wide open first-quarter threes to Toronto's supporting cast. Beating the Warriors is all about massaging the math. Threes are worth more than twos, and no one in the history bombs triples the way Klay Thompson and Steph Curry have since the Warriors' ascent. Even though the Raptors fired up 14 triples in the first quarter, connecting on five, you could have still quibbled with a couple long balls the likes of Marc Gasol and Kyle Lowry opted to pass up.

The point though, is that those threes were available, and it was all thanks to Leonard's magnetism. Earlier in the postseason, selling out the stop Leonard might have been a usable strategy against Philadelphia or for the first couple games against the Bucks, when if the supporting cast wasn't bricking shots it was straight up passing out of them. The equation changes when Pascal Siakam, Marc Gasol, and Danny Green can swish 7-of-16 triples combined as they did in Game 1.

"It's not Kawhi Leonard. It's the Raptors." said Klay Thompson after the game in assessment of Golden State's Kawhi-focused D. Imagine hearing that back in round two.

More crucial than anyone else to Toronto's from-all-angles attack in Game 1 was Pascal Siakam. Toronto's ascendant star saw his efficiency gradually slashed over the course of the postseason, as the defenders in his grill got progressively more daunting. It speaks to how exponentially his development curve exploded in such a short time that the Sixers and Bucks assigned their best defenders — Embiid and Antetokounmpo — to the cause of slowing down Siakam. After dealing with the league's two closest things to real life Monstars, Siakam seemed positively giddy at the sight of former Defensive Player of the Year Draymond Green and his ho hum 6'7 frame.

Siakam's first quarter oozed comfortability. He attacked mismatches when they presented themselves, but was as at home driving and spinning around Green

as he was against the overmatched Curry. He left the opening frame with a tidy five points, two rebounds, and three assists on his ledger. It was in the second half where Siakam really invited himself to the center of the NBA's grandest stage.

Here's a quick rundown of Siakam's exploits on a string of consecutive possessions to begin the third quarter:

- A silky spin move and a bucket around Green
- A mid-range jumper than rattled in
- A trip to the free-throw line and a pair of makes
- His fourth assist of the night on an acrobatic leap and dump off to a charging Leonard on the break
- A sublime switch out onto Klay Thompson that helped force a Warriors shot clock violation
- A driving, banked-in hook shot out of the left corner
- Another wide-receiver like catch in traffic that he flipped into a finger-roll finish
- Another pull-up 20-footer

All of this happened in the first six minutes of the quarter.

By the time of the final buzzer, Siakam sat on 32 points to pair with eight rebounds, five assists, a steal, and two blocks on a blazing 82 percent from the field — quite literally one of the best Finals performances turned in by anyone, ever. Between the second and fourth quarters, 11-straight Siakam shots found mesh; he even recovered his lone second half miss and put it back to all but seal the win in closing time.

"He's made himself into a guy," said Draymond Green of Siakam's performance, taking blame for allowing the 25-year-old to go off. "He put a lot of work in to get there and I respect that. But … I gotta take him outta this series and that's on me."

Siakam, as well as Danny Green, Gasol (20 points on 6-of-10 shooting), and Fred VanVleet (15 points on 5-of-8) proved a couple things in the Finals opener. First, that the Raptors could in fact survive relative off nights from Leonard and Kyle Lowry (they shot a combined 7-of-23

Pascal Siakam attacks the basket with Draymond Green defending. Siakam was spectacular in the Game 1 win, with 32 points, eight rebounds, and five assists.

in the win), and second, that Toronto's secondary guys were very much not afraid of the brightest lights.

How could they be, really? On the road to Game 1, Toronto had faced just about every adverse situation in the book. All the Raptors had seen and overcome was the seasoning they needed to take on challenge of the two-time champs with eagerness instead of fear. Having Kawhi Leonard's unbreakable calm hanging around the room can't have hurt, either.

"We know that they're human. I mean they're a great basketball team, talented players, high basketball IQ players," Kawhi said after the win. "You just gotta go out there and compete, take the challenge. We know they're gonna make big shots, go on runs. It's about just keeping your composure and keep fighting through, don't put your head down. Players like Steph or Klay make big threes, just keep playing."

Just keep playing. Successfully abide Leonard's advice three more times, and the title would be coming North. ∎

Warriors 109, Raptors 104
June 2, 2019 • Toronto, Ontario

COUNTERPUNCH

Warriors Overtake Raptors with Third Quarter Onslaught, Tie Series

By Sean Woodley

In the aftermath of Game 1 of The Finals, Draymond Green accepted culpability for the Warriors' failings — particularly when it came to wrangling Toronto's galloping transition weapon, Pascal Siakam.

"I think he played an amazing game obviously, but he got out in transition and our transition D was horrible, and I let him get in a rhythm in the first half, first quarter really," said the former Defensive Player of the Year. "So I got to do a better job of taking his rhythm away, and I will, but he had a great game … He's become a guy. He put a lot of work in to get there and I respect that, but like I said, I got to take him out of the series and that's on me."

No finger-pointing, no befuddlement over the schooling he'd just received at Siakam's hands; just acceptance and acknowledgement of the need to be better, and an ominous tone alluded to the adjustments to come. Siakam shot 5-of-18 in Game 2, by the way.

Draymond's displeasure with his effort in the opener was echoed by his teammates. The Warriors weren't happy to see their flawless record in Finals Game 1s besmirched. Green mentioned Klay Thompson as one Warrior who was especially peeved.

"Klay's not one to just walk around showing emotion, but you kind of get, you can get a feel for when he is [ticked] off. I got that feeling," Green said on the ever of Game 2. "You could just see it when he was walking off the floor (after Game 1). Like, there's a certain bounce that he has."

Anyone who didn't think that bounce foretold a swift Warriors strike-back in Game 2 hadn't been paying attention for the previous five years. How prepared Toronto was to absorb the blow was the only real uncertainty heading into Sunday night at Scotiabank Arena.

Early returns were promising from a Toronto perspective. The Raptors defense stayed swarming. Apart from a revenge-seeking, en fuego Thompson registering 11 first quarter points, the Warriors shot poorly. Steph Curry, reportedly dealing with a bout of dehydration, started out bucketless on three attempts, saved only by four made free throws. Seven of eight Raptors to see the court scored in the first 12 minutes, and Toronto escaped the quarter with a 27-26 lead.

The second quarter passed without a Warriors tsunami, too. Even in the face of foul trouble for Kyle Lowry, Toronto padded its lead. Fred VanVleet added more pages to his folk hero's tale. He joined Kawhi Leonard as the only Raptors in double figures in the half. He'd finish with 17 points in a tenacious 38 minutes of action.

Game 2 lacked the flow you'd traditionally see from the Raptors and Warriors. If foul calls didn't outnumber uninterrupted possessions, it was darn close. Through the charity of the whistle and a missed three by Norman Powell that would have opened up a 14-point Toronto lead, the Warriors crept uncomfortably close — within five points — with the third quarter on tap.

Golden State's propensity for life-sapping third quarter runs had long been canon before the second half of Game 2 in Toronto. They'd overcome double-digit Portland leads in the back 24 minutes of the final three games of their sweep of Blazers the round prior. Everyone in attendance for Game 2 knew what to expect next. Anticipation didn't make the next six minutes any less awe-inspiring.

Over a stretch spanning five minutes and forty seconds, five forced turnovers, and two Raptors timeouts, the Warriors rattled off 18 unanswered points. Using Curry's floor-bending gravity as an off-ball screener, Golden State unleashed a parade of dunks and layups. Death by a dozen back cuts. DeMarcus Cousins, making his first start since returning from a month and half on the shelf, picked out those cutters with rust-free precision. Golden State's 34 assists on 38 buckets was the highest assist percentage posted by any team in a Finals game since 1960. All 22 of their second half makes had an accompanying dime. Toronto's usually adaptable defense seemed unprepared for the onslaught.

"Yeah, I mean, it was the big point in the game. I thought just staying in the game at the end of the second quarter was also very important," Steve Kerr said of the way the Warriors flipped the game. "I think we were down 12 and the place was going nuts, we couldn't score, and Steph and Klay both got loose and the game loosened up a little bit and we scored. We weren't exactly making stops, but we cut the lead to five and could kind of breathe at halftime.

"I think our guys felt renewed life at that point and came out and just had a great run to take control of the game, and we were able to finish it out from there."

To a man, the Raptors placed blame on their porous offense for putting the defense in an unenviable spot.

"They jumped out on us and it was hard to get back set after that," said VanVleet. "You got to score against this team, I mean 21 points in the third quarter is not going to do it, and our offense has got to be better. And I think that probably adds an extra 10 on their side."

In yet another showcase of Toronto's now fabled resilience, it survived the bludgeoning without falling too far out of touch. Leonard made use of a favorable whistle and racked up free throws in lieu of a functioning Raptors half court attack. Eight points didn't feel insurmountable with 12 minutes left to play. Leonard looked to be entering takeover mode, 28 of his eventual 34 points already in the bag.

A frantic sequence of events to open the fourth left both sides spinning. Quinn Cook and Danny Green traded threes, because the playoffs are weird. Klay Thompson injured his hamstring trying to collect a three-point shooting foul, because the playoffs are cruel. He joined Kevon Looney (shoulder) among Warriors to leave the game unable to return.

With the Raptors desperate for stops, and the Warriors running low on warm bodies, things got especially bizarre in the final six minutes. Nick Nurse pulled a trick out of the high school coaches' bag and deployed a box-and-one zone defense — four guys in a square inside the arc, and a lone, roving Steph Curry pest (Fred VanVleet) scurrying about above the arc. The goal: dare anyone but Curry to launch up low-percentage threes. And it … worked?

Toronto took its turn holding their opponent to a 5-minute scoreless stretch, and the Raptors cut the lead from 12 to two — though a handful of uncontested misses left Nurse wanting more. Kyle Lowry also fouled out on a silly swipe at DeMarcus Cousins' hands. Not ideal.

"Well, I was feeling really good because we stopped their scoring, right, and finally got something figured out there to slow them down," Nurse said of his funky defensive alignment. "And we were getting a bunch of wide-open shots, I think we missed three wide-open threes in a row there to cut it to maybe four, right, and maybe it was five … a bunch of stops in a row and we didn't get much to show for it at the other end."

With 26 seconds to play and the score 106-104, the scenario was a tricky one to navigate for the Raptors. Rather than foul and draw out the game, the Raptors opted to try to force a steal. They nearly did, before a sure-handed Shaun Livingston picked out an unmanned Andre Iguodala. He rose up, and drained the dagger that sent the series back to Oakland tied at 1-1.

Curry called Toronto's abandonment of Iguodala "disrespectful" in his post-game walk-off interview with ESPN's Doris Burke.

"Well, we weren't disrespecting anybody," retorted Nurse. "We were up guarding hard, and we put two on Steph and he almost threw it right to Kawhi, right? It was pretty good defense, they were scrambling around, running around like crazy."

To be disrespectful of the Warriors is to be impossibly stupid. Toronto certainly was not that. Golden State threw the counterpunch that had been telegraphed since Thursday, but they left the second bout battered. Thompson's hamstring, Iguodala's quad, Looney's shoulder, Kevin Durant's persistent calf injury — all threatened to derail Golden State in segments of Game 2. Just as much as the Raptors, the Warriors would be in survival mode for Game 3. Only 96 minutes played and already, what a series. ■

NBA FINALS, GAME 3

Raptors 123, Warriors 109
June 5, 2019 • Oakland, California

OPPORTUNITY KNOCKS

Raptors Take Advantage of Warriors' Injuries and Take Back Homecourt with Game 3 Win

By Alex Wong

Opportunity.

It is a word used by players around the league often, especially in the postseason. The opportunity to win an NBA championship comes around only so often. For many players, they spend an entire career chasing that goal without ever coming close. For the Toronto Raptors, the door to their first ever title opened ever so slightly before Game 3, when the Golden State Warriors announced Klay Thompson would be out with a hamstring injury. Adding to the injuries keeping Kevin Durant and Kevon Looney on the sidelines, suddenly the Raptors were in the driver seat on the road, with a chance to regain control of the series.

The Warriors are two-time defending champions and even with a depleted roster, were not about to just hand Toronto a victory at Oracle Arena, especially not when Steph Curry was still on the floor, a one-man offense unto himself. Toronto knew coming into the game Curry would be the focal point of their attack, and were still helpless for most of the night. Curry scored 17 points in the first quarter en route to a masterful performance: 47 points, eight rebounds, and seven assists in 43 minutes.

Despite Curry's incredible night, it was Toronto who took control of the game early, seizing the opportunity against an undermanned Golden State team, taking an eight-point lead into the locker room at halftime. After losing the third quarter 34-21 in Game 2, head coach Nick Nurse made an adjustment to start the second half in Game 3, sending starting shooting guard Danny Green to the bench and inserting Fred VanVleet into the starting lineup to start the third.

The move was made to provide some on-ball pressure on Curry, and while the Warriors guard still managed to score 15 points in the quarter, VanVleet was able to limit Golden State from going on a game-changing run. On the other end of the floor, the Raptors found their rhythm from beyond the arc, making 17 three-pointers, tying the NBA Finals record for most three-pointers made on the road.

All five starters scored in double digits. Kyle Lowry bounced back from a subpar performance in Game 2 to pour in 23 points while adding nine assists. Danny Green broke out of his postseason shooting slump with six three-pointers. Pascal Siakam had 18 points, nine rebounds, and six assists. Marc Gasol played his best game of the series, outdueling DeMarcus Cousins to the tune of 17 points and seven rebounds. Kawhi Leonard also had his best game of the series, finishing with 30 points, seven rebounds, and six assists.

The Raptors surround Golden State guard Stephen Curry in the paint. Curry had 47 points, eight rebounds, and seven assists, but the Raptors limited his teammates and took a 2-1 series lead.

Golden State's motto during their championship run has been Strength in Numbers, to illustrate the power of the overall group that is required to win a title. On this night, it was the Raptors who borrowed this slogan.

The starters carried the way, but in the fourth quarter, two reserves got a chance to shine. Serge Ibaka struggled for most of the evening but was huge on the defensive end in the final 12 minutes, and recorded six blocks in his 22 minutes of play. With 1:39 left in the game, the Warriors still managed to hang around thanks to Curry's scoring barrage, but VanVleet drilled a three-pointer at the end of the shot clock to put the Raptors up 13, and send the Oracle Arena fans to the exits. The Raptors completed an all-around professional performance on the road, winning 123-109.

Afterwards, the Raptors were quick to shower praise on all of their teammates. "He was great tonight," Siakam said of Lowry. "Just controlling the pace and also finding his shots and looking to score. When he does both of those things and also the hustle plays on defense, I think that's the whole package for Kyle. Having him on the squad is definitely something that we cherish. He's our floor general."

Lowry gave credit to Nurse for his adjustments and ability to put players in a position to succeed. "His mind for the game has been special," Lowry told reporters afterwards. "The growth throughout the year has been pretty good for him. He's not a first-time head coach, he's a first time NBA head coach, but the experience that he's had in his many leagues and teams that he's been a head coach before, he's kind of just stepped up and continued to grow with that."

Leonard, the even-keeled leader of the team, was more matter-of-fact about what the Game 3 victory meant. "Another step closer to our goal," Leonard told reporters afterwards.

A road victory in the postseason is always special, but especially so for this Raptors team, who know how well their fans travel during the playoffs. After the win, a small contingent of fans remained at the arena and started "Let's Go Raptors" chants and even broke into the singing of the "O Canada" national anthem.

"All around the world there's Canadian fans," Green told reporters afterwards. "That's the one thing I learned being on this team, a lot of Canada is all over, and it's kind of close. People from Vancouver may drive down. But Raptors fans are crazy, man. They're all over the place and they come from all over the place to watch the games and to support us."

The fervor across Canada for the Toronto Raptors will only grow now. With Game 3's win, they're now two victories away from their first ever NBA championship. ■

Kyle Lowry bounced back from a quiet Game 2 with 23 points and nine assists in the Game 3 win.

Raptors 105, Warriors 92
June 7, 2019 • Oakland, California

ROAD WARRIORS

Raptors Take Commanding Series Lead, Stand One Win Away from Title

By Alex Wong

With a chance to take a commanding 3-1 lead in the NBA Finals, Toronto needed to first weather the storm at the start of Game 4. The Warriors responded as champions do, coming out of the gate with more desperation and energy than the Raptors. Early on, Toronto could not get a single shot to fall and fell behind by six points after 12 minutes. They shot 29 percent from the field in the quarter, and needed 14 points from Kawhi Leonard to avoid an insurmountable deficit.

The second quarter didn't start any better. The Raptors missed all seven of their three-point attempts in the period, and after a hot shooting Game 3, made just 2-of-17 from beyond the arc in the first half of Game 4. Toronto leaned on its defense to keep them in the game. Despite 14 points from Klay Thompson in the first half, the Raptors dialed up their defensive intensity and somehow only trailed 46-42 heading into halftime.

And then, a third quarter explosion came to put the Raptors on the brink of their first NBA championship. On the first two possessions of the quarter, Leonard took command and made two three-pointers to pull Toronto ahead. Their shots started to fall, and as the offense started rolling, their defense refused to let up. The Oracle Arena crowd was stunned by a 37-21 push from Toronto

in the third that had them up 12 points headed into the fourth quarter.

As time ticked away late in the game, the Raptors refused to surrender their lead, and had a response for every time the Warriors appeared to threaten. Toronto seemed to get fresher legs as the game went on, while Golden State appeared very much like a short-handed team exhausted from having to keep up with Toronto's relentlessness on both ends of the floor. A three-pointer from Steph Curry cut the Raptors lead to eight points with 2:56 remaining, but it was the closest Golden State would get. Toronto took care of business in the final minutes, hitting key shots, making the right rotations on defense, and calmly nailing their free throws to put the game away.

The final score: 105-92 Raptors.

Toronto got a game-high 36 points and 12 rebounds from Leonard, who helped lead the team to two consecutive road wins in the NBA Finals. Serge Ibaka was huge coming off the bench with 20 points on 9-for-12 shooting in 22 minutes.

Fred VanVleet left the game in the fourth quarter after catching an inadvertent elbow to the face from Shaun Livingston, and finished with eight points in 29 minutes, and credited Leonard's two three-pointers

Marc Gasol and Golden State's Draymond Green battle for the rebound during the first half of Toronto's Game 4 win. Gasol had nine points, seven rebounds, and three assists in the road win.

coming out of halftime as a momentum changer.

"Kawhi came out and hit two big … shots to start the half," VanVleet told reporters after the game. "There's no defense for that. There are no schemes for that. That's two big-boy shots that he came out of the half with, two back-to-back threes. And that just kind of let you know how we were going to approach the third quarter and the rest of the half. It put us in good position."

In a game many expected the Warriors to win, it was Toronto who had a championship response after looking shaky in the early goings. The Raptors are surely thrilled about going home with a 3-1 lead, but nobody is satisfied yet. The job isn't done. Once again, it was Leonard who has set the tone for this team throughout the playoffs, who made everyone aware of the task that remains.

"It's not over yet," Leonard said. "So I can't say that we're better. Just the key to tonight's win was pretty much, as you guys know, playing defense. And towards that second half we started to make some shots, and we just pretty much stuck into the game, stayed in the game."

Kyle Lowry echoed those sentiments.

"We didn't do nothing yet," Lowry said. "We haven't done anything. We won three games. It's the first of four. We understand that. They're the defending champs, and they're not going to go out easy. They're going to come and fight and prepare to play the next game, and that's how we're preparing ourselves, that we have to — we got to prepare ourselves to play the next game. We haven't done anything yet."

In a playoff run full of improbable moments, the Raptors delivered one more by winning both games at Oracle Arena in Games 3 and 4.

Now, they stand one victory away from winning the first championship in franchise history. ∎

Danny Green (left) and Serge Ibaka (right) defend Golden State guard Stephen Curry. Curry scored 27 points in the game but took 22 shots in the process.

NBA FINALS, GAME 5

Warriors 106, Raptors 105
June 10, 2019 • Toronto, Ontario

SHELL-SHOCKED

Raptors Let Clinching Opportunity Slip, While Warriors Prolong Series but Lose Durant

By Sean Woodley

While the Larry O'Brien trophy was in the house for Game 5 of the NBA Finals, the energy inside Scotiabank Arena was anything but celebratory. Golden State's 106-105 win would go down as one of the most bizarre, emotionally taxing, competitive, and ultimately disappointing Finals games in history.

At the epicentre of the angst that plagued the evening was Kevin Durant.

In the lead up to the first elimination game of the series back in Toronto, Durant's status was the topic du jour three days running. If he was ever going to return from the calf strain that had held him out since Game 5 of the second round, a game going into which the Warriors trailed 3-1 would be the time. Reports of frustration within the team over the uncertainty regarding his return quickly faded into news that he'd practice the day before the game. In the hours before tip-off, Durant's availability for Game 5 was confirmed. A city accustomed to the things that could go wrong in fact going wrong clenched in unison.

Toronto's Durant-inspired fear proved to be unfounded, in the most disheartening way possible. With 11 points on five shots to his name, the Warriors leading 39-34, and 10 minutes to go in the second quarter, Durant got stripped by Serge Ibaka on a crossover attempt. As Ibaka sprinted the other way, Durant fell to the floor holding his right Achilles. His expression was one of resigned understanding. It would later be passed on by Warriors president Bob Myers that it was an Achilles injury and an MRI later confirmed that it ruptured.

"He was cleared to play tonight; that was a collaborative decision," said Myers at the post-game podium, fighting back tears. "I don't believe there's anybody to blame, but I understand in this world and if you have to, you can blame me. I run our basketball operations department."

"And to tell you something about Kevin Durant, Kevin Durant loves to play basketball, and the people that questioned whether he wanted to get back to this team were wrong."

Whether it was the shock of seeing Durant go down, or the icky stench left behind by the fragments of the home crowd who cheered in response to his departure — some courtside morons even mockingly waved goodbye as he was carried off by his teammates — Scotiabank Arena's life was zapped. From the doldrums rose some incensed champs.

Even down Durant, the two-time defending champions were never going to go away quietly. Too much sweat equity had gone in their five-year run of making the Finals to cave in an elimination game, healthy or not. In the minutes after Durant's departure, the Warriors ripped off a 12-4 run that tossed the Raptors into a 13-point hole. DeMarcus Cousins, borderline unplayable in Games 3 and 4, chipped in an essential nine points and five rebounds in the first half. A Steph Curry four-point play capped the run, and also spurred on a patented Raptors counterpunch.

Kyle Lowry, ever the Raptors' engine, started to run. Stringing together steal after steal, fast break upon fast break, Toronto trimmed the Warriors lead to 62-56 heading into a second half upon which the narrative of the series would hinge. Either the Raptors would complete their run to history, or the Warriors would force a Game 6 in Oakland, with a poetic comeback from down 3-1 still on the table.

After such a disjointed and sullen opening 24 minutes, the second half was much needed palate cleanser. More than any other segment of the series, the final two quarters of Game 5 were a display of riveting competition between two teams exuding equal desperation; this was what Finals basketball is supposed to be.

Golden State cocked back the first haymaker of the half. A continuation of the game's vast three-point disparity saw the Warriors jump back out to a 14-point lead, 77-63, in the opening six minutes of the quarter. At that juncture, the Warriors had canned 14 of their 26 attempts from three; Toronto was just 3-for-18. Unlike earlier games in the series, Toronto wasn't funneling long range attempts to the Warriors array of shaky shooters. It was two of the greatest shooters of all time comprising the bulk of the volume.

"I think the fact that Steph and Klay were able to get off 14 and 13 threes is too many," Kyle Lowry said after the game. "They got off way too many threes. For guys like them, they're going to make — you give them that many threes, they're going to make some."

If there's one thing the Raptors had proven throughout the postseason, it's that they'd never seen a double-digit deficit they couldn't make up. Once again, it was Lowry who led the next Toronto response, as he took it upon himself to oil up a squeaky offense. Without mercy, he put Golden State's big men on their heels, carving out space for himself and his shooters in the process. Toronto cut the lead to a manageable six points going into the fourth quarter, a title in the balance.

Kawhi Leonard had been the Mariano Rivera of the playoffs. In tight games, he was as sure a thing as you could find to close them out. For a time in the fourth quarter of Game 5, it appeared as though he might come up with his most dramatic and important save of his near-flawless spring. What made Leonard's fourth quarter so impressive was his not-so-stellar opening 36 minutes. Through three frames he'd posted just 14 points on 4-of-12 shooting. An errant pass to an empty corner late in the third highlighted his discomfort with the Warriors' swarming defense. He shook off the restraints in the fourth.

Lowry and Ibaka set the table for Leonard's finishing flourish to start the quarter. Lowry, playing at peak jitterbug levels, continued to slice the Warriors up, routinely finding an amped up Ibaka for easy buckets around the rim. With the score 92-91 Golden State, Leonard took the helm.

Over a stretch of three pandemonic minutes, Leonard grabbed an offensive board and converted a put back, assisted a graceful Norman Powell transition dunk, canned a pull-up three, stuck an eight-footer, and buried two more absolutely roof-rocking triples. After a seven-point swing orchestrated entirely by the future Finals MVP, Toronto led 103-97. Toronto could taste its first ring; the building was shaking as such.

It was a little perplexing, then, when the Raptors called a timeout off a Warriors miss with 3:05 to play and the arena in an absolute tizzy. Nick Nurse explained the roll-slowing decision at the post-game podium.

"Yeah, well, we had two free ones that you lose under the three-minute mark," Nurse began. "And we just came across and just decided to give those guys a rest, and we had back-to-back ones there that we would have lost them under the three-minute mark, and just thought we could use the extra energy push."

Instead, the Warriors were the ones nudged forward by the stoppage. Draymond Green even mentioned after the game that the timeout helped Golden State regroup. In those final three minutes and five seconds, Toronto never saw the ball go through the basket again. Wrapped around a DeMarcus Cousins goaltending violation came three triples in the face of good defense by Thompson and Curry, the guys who make a living off hitting threes in the face of good defense. Some clunky Raptors possessions — including a missed Lowry three and a backcourt violation — left Toronto trailing by one with 15 seconds on the clock and the ball under the Golden State basket.

Fred VanVleet brought the ball up the floor and dished it to Leonard, who drove into a Thompson-Andre Iguodala double team, forcing a swing to Lowry in the weak side corner. With a championship on his fingertips, Lowry rose up and fired, but the outstretched hand of Draymond Green grazed it just enough to send it wayward. Game over. Back to Oakland.

All told, while the disappointment of a failed closeout attempt was palpable, the loss may have been a bit of a blessing. Durant's injury cast a sad fog over the game; the response of Toronto's fans aligned the cosmos against a Raptors triumph. Hoisting the trophy under those circumstances would have tasted sour, if not entirely tainted. Toronto would have to wait 72 hours for another chance at making history. Game 6 would, hopefully, be more worthy of a championship celebration. ∎

NBA FINALS, GAME 6

Raptors 114, Warriors 110
June 13, 2019 • Oakland, California

THE 6 IN GAME 6!

Raptors Claim NBA Crown After Knocking Off Two-Time Defending Champion Warriors

By Alex Wong

Even with 0.9 seconds left on the clock in a game that had finally been decided, the moment didn't feel real. The Toronto Raptors, the franchise that spent over two decades getting to this point, was finally on the verge of becoming NBA champions.

Eliminating the Golden State Warriors was never going to be an easy task. In Game 5, the Raptors had the championship within their grasp at home, leading by six with just over three minutes left in the fourth quarter, and watched Steph Curry and Klay Thompson extend the series with their offensive brilliance.

The same story appeared to be playing out in Game 6, the final game ever at Oracle Arena. Even without Kevin Durant and with Klay Thompson leaving the game in the third quarter due to injury, the Warriors kept coming. In a back-and-forth affair, neither team ever pulled away by double digits, with lead changes coming in bunches. The Warriors refused to go away, and the Raptors were staring at a Game 7 at home with all the pressure on them.

And then, an unlikely hero. Just three years ago, Fred VanVleet went undrafted and made the Raptors team out of training camp. Steadily, he improved his game and earned the trust of his coaches, before he became one of the top bench players in the league last season. And then, in a potential Finals clinching road game, the Rockford, Illinois native stepped up, making five three-pointers and scoring 22 points, helping to steady Toronto's offense repeatedly.

It was another complete effort from the Raptors. Kyle Lowry scored the team's first 11 points in the first quarter and finished with 26 points. Pascal Siakam, who grew by leaps and bounds throughout the season, added 26 points himself. Kawhi Leonard didn't have a dominant game, but still pitched in with 22 points in a winning effort.

The final seconds finally ticked away, and the scoreboard read 114-110 for the Raptors. The Toronto Raptors, your 2018-19 NBA champions.

When the season started back at training camp in September, there was excitement but also uncertainty. After winning the championship, Leonard revealed the plan all along. "I texted Kyle [Lowry] probably a day later, or the day that I got traded and told him I said let's go out and do something special," Leonard said. "I know your best friend left, I know you're mad, but let's make this thing work out. And we are here today."

The Raptors overcame adversity throughout the playoffs, trailing in every single series prior to the NBA Finals. Against the short-handed Warriors, it became increasingly clear as the series went along that Toronto was the better team, but they still needed to get to four

Kyle Lowry lead the charge in Game 6 with 26 points, 10 assists, and seven rebounds to help secure the Raptors' 114-110 win.

wins to make it count. It wasn't easy, but the Raptors proved they had championship mettle, winning all three games on the road in the series.

"It was a heck of a 12 months," head coach Nick Nurse told reporters afterwards. "And I don't know, I just try to take things as they come. Didn't look too far ahead. Obviously when we made some additions to the team, we thought we could be good, but we had no idea what the health status was and all those things."

The Raptors have disappointed their fans in the postseason before but in these playoffs, they made their fanbase believe. A veteran group came together and overcame every single obstacle in their path.

"Two months of playoff basketball, they never seemed tired to me," Nurse said. "Mentally they kept wanting film sessions, they kept wanting to walk through things, they kept wanting to keep learning and improving. And I think that was a big key because we had to do that in the playoff run because we really hadn't had all that much time together."

"It's a top-class organization. They're all about winning," Marc Gasol told reporters after the game. "It doesn't guarantee you're going to win, but it does help that everyone has that championship mentality. I'm so happy that they got it because everyone in Toronto and Canada deserves this because they fought for it. I'm sure the Jurassic Park is going a little crazy right now; I just hope everybody is okay. But I'm sure there's a lot of people very happy, because we have shown a lot of resilience and togetherness."

They all came together and played their part. And now the 2018-19 Toronto Raptors can call themselves NBA champions forever. ∎

Fred VanVleet rose to the occasion in Game 6, breaking out for 22 clutch points while playing tough defense on Stephen Curry.

BOARD MAN GETS TITLES

Finals MVP Kawhi Leonard Credits Group Effort

By Sean Woodley

Kawhi Leonard's whole vibe is understated. It's not as though he avoids the spotlight; he just seems unaltered by its bright shininess. A total of 283 thousand people follow his Twitter account, from which he has posted exactly four times, all during a seven-month span of 2015, and never since. He is the king of the casual 30-point outing, accruing loud scoring totals without so much as a peep on the floor. For Leonard, everything looks easy.

So then maybe it's no surprise that he walked into the second Finals MVP honor of his career simply by showing up to the NBA Finals and being Kawhi Leonard.

His grasp over the series tightened over time. After Toronto's Game 1 victory, he wasn't even the early favourite to earn the Finals' top honour. A line of 23 points, eight rebounds, and five assists — ho hum by Leonard's ludicrous standards — was outdone by Pascal Siakam's 32-8-5 on a blazing 14-of-17 from the floor.

Leonard would settle in as the series progressed. At the times when the Warriors flashed glimpses of their best selves, Leonard was the Raptors' emergency break.

As his teammates and coach had alluded to throughout Toronto's dramatic run to the championship, his steadiness seeped into the DNA of the entire team. A franchise once derided for its frailty in big moments morphed into a team as unflappable and workmanlike as its star.

Prior to Game 5 of the Finals, coach Nick Nurse was asked about the team's resolve to grab wins in Games 3 and 4, both on the road, after leaving home with a disappointing 1-1 split

"Well, I give most of that credit to Kawhi, because I said it in the locker room trying to kind of not make it feel so bad that we just lost a home game in the Finals," Nurse said. "I was like, 'All we got to do is go get one,' that's maybe not an insurmountable challenge to go out there and get one."

"And Kawhi said, 'Let's go get them both.'"

They got them both. Leonard averaged 33 points, 9.5 rebounds, and four assists over the two wins at Oracle Arena.

In Game 5, the MVP recovered from a so-so opening three quarters to nearly clinch the series on his own. A Leonard-powered 12-2 run in the fourth put the Raptors up six with three minutes to play. Championship hats and tees were ready to be dispensed, the locker room was lined with champagne-proof plastic, and MVP award presenter Bill Russell was on stand-by before the Warriors saved their season. Leonard would have to wait to shake Russell's hand for a few more days.

Their joyous meeting took place after Game 6, wherein Leonard concluded his run in his typically understated fashion. The attention Leonard demanded from Golden State's defense all series long granted his teammates space to clinch Game 6. Leonard's 22 points were earned in the gaps between the explosions of Lowry (26 points), Fred VanVleet (22), and Pascal Siakam (26).

"Obviously I didn't come out in this series trying to

Kawhi Leonard lifts the Bill Russell NBA Finals Most Valuable Player Award after Game 6.

win it," Leonard said of the award he'd just been granted. "It was a whole group collectively. Tonight, Fred played amazing in that fourth. Kyle played amazing tonight throughout the whole game. Pascal played big. I just kept striving and pushing and I ended up with the trophy, but everybody deserves it."

The clincher proved to be Leonard's calmly drawn exclamation point to close off one of the most dazzling wire-to-wire postseason performances in league history. His first Finals MVP came at the expense of the Miami Heat's attempted three-peat in 2014. His second kept the Warriors from doing the same thing.

Kawhi Leonard: dynasty stopper, two-time Finals MVP. ■

ROAD TO THE CHAMPIONSHIP

PRIMED AND READY

The Raptors Spent the Season Building Chemistry and Tweaking the Roster, Setting the Stage for a Historic Run

By Sean Woodley

Even for a previously moribund franchise like the Toronto Raptors, the established formula set out by the teams led by Kyle Lowry, DeMar DeRozan, and coach Dwane Casey over the previous five seasons had grown stale. After a third-straight playoff exit at the hands of LeBron James' Cavaliers — the latest of which being the most utterly heart-wrenching yet — team president Masai Ujiri faced a fundamental question centered around the goals of himself and the team under his charge: stick with the group that reliably owned the regular season but was prone to dramatic postseason flame-outs, or shake up the core behind the only prolonged run of success Raptors fans had ever known?

Ujiri, never a man content with being merely good, would opt for the latter.

UJIRI GOES ALL-IN

Ujiri's first move was to change the dynamic on the bench. Casey had won more games than any other Raptors coach by a long shot, and had proven to be among the best culture-builders in the entire league. But seven years after Casey's arrival, the Raptors had outgrown the need for an organizational pillar. Toronto needed a tactician — someone more willing to deviate from a successful regular season script when the playoff gauntlet challenged it. After a lengthy search, Ujiri landed on long-time Casey assistant and basketball world-traveller, Nick Nurse.

About six weeks after his June hiring, Nurse was gifted a new toy.

The season-long feud between the San Antonio Spurs and their injured (?) star Kawhi Leonard in 2017-18 created a unique opportunity upon which Ujiri could pounce. Typically a star of Leonard's ilk — a former Finals MVP and two-time top-three finisher in MVP voting — would command an enormous return in a trade; high picks, young stars, you name it. With just a year remaining on his contract and a veil of uncertainty surrounding his health status, Leonard's price was diminished, meaning the Raptors could afford it. As a team that had skinned every last morsel of potential from its core, and Lowry inching into his mid-30s, Toronto could soak up some risk in exchange for a short-term upgrade.

In the wee hours of July 18th, 2018, reports started filtering in that the Raptors were making their move. ESPN's Adrian Wojnarowski confirmed the terms of the Leonard trade later that morning. Kawhi Leonard and longtime teammate Danny Green were North-bound; fan favourite DeRozan, backup centre Jakob Poeltl, and a protected first-round pick were sent the other way.

Rumours swirled that Leonard had no interest in playing for the Raptors. DeRozan expressed his disapproval with the way the move was sprung on him via Instagram. Fans who had invested nine years in DeRozan's ascent from toolsy dunker to perennial All-Star feared the team had traded away its most loyal player for a mercenary who would leave the way Chris Bosh, Vince Carter, and Damon Stoudamire had done before, if he ever showed up at all. A photo released of Leonard with Ujiri and general manager Bobby Webster later that week calmed those tensions.

At a somewhat awkward media day unveiling of Leonard and Green, Ujiri pleaded with Raptors fans to believe in the ability of the city and franchise to make a compelling pitch to Leonard to stick around for more than just one year.

Masai Ujiri (right) hired Nick Nurse (left) in June 2018, beginning the reshaping of the Raptors into a championship franchise.

"The narrative of not wanting to come to this city is gone," said Ujiri. "I think that's old and we should move past that. Believe in this city, believe in yourself. We can stop talking about coming to the city or wanting to come to the city, that's old talk. We want to win."

EARLY RETURNS

Any lingering fan trepidation about the deal was swatted away the moment folks saw what Leonard was capable of. In the second game of the year against the pre-season Eastern Conference favourite Boston Celtics, the refurbished Raptors flashed an early glimpse of the championship-level machine it could be. After three narrowly-contested quarters, Toronto ripped off the first of many stretches of smothering, game-sealing defense it would string together over the course of the season.

This particular instance of defensive asphyxia was capped off by Green and Leonard combining for a double-block on Boston's Jayson Tatum in transition. Leonard finished with 31 points, 10 rebounds, and three assists in the 113-101 win, and received MVP chants from the quickly won over Toronto faithful.

"It's a little too early," Leonard said of the mid-October chants. "I appreciate the support. I know they're excited about us winning the game tonight."

Even with Leonard on a strict health regimen that saw him sit out half of every set of back-to-back games, the Raptors cruised to a 12-1 record out of the gate. Dissenters of the trade piped down quickly.

TESTING THE METTLE (X2)

Toronto faced little resistance during its torrid start to the season. Signature wins over Boston and Philadelphia didn't exactly stand out against a crowded backdrop of wins over lottery-bound sad sacks. Losses in a rematch with the Celtics and in Dwane Casey's emotionally-charged return with the Pistons to Toronto left some question about the realness of the Raptors when the champs, Golden State, came to town on November 29th.

Steph Curry and Draymond Green missed the game with injury, but Kevin Durant's 51-point turn as

a superhero ensured the Warriors were a more than formidable opponent. Toronto survived KD's onslaught, with Leonard's 37 points on 14-of-24 from the field leading the way. Toronto moved to a very real 19-4.

The rematch came 13 days later in Oakland, although it being a back-to-back for Toronto, Leonard did not partake. It didn't matter. Kyle Lowry orchestrated a quick-fire Raptors attack with 23 points and 12 assists, and the Warriors never made it especially close. Toronto strolled to a 113-93 win to move to 23-7. It was not a casualty free win, however. Centre Jonas Valanciunas badly injured his thumb in the first half. Unbeknownst to everyone at the time was that it would be the final game he'd play in a Raptors uniform.

Toronto had now beaten Golden State twice — once with a Leonard bucket frenzy, the second time around with an all-hands effort minus Leonard. The wins shed light on one of the underlying tensions of the 2018-19 Raptors. On offense, the team had yet to congeal. Too often, Toronto would oscillate between a Leonard-led, ISO-heavy attack, and a more vibrant and free motion offense when Leonard would sit and Kyle Lowry, fully bought in as an assist-slinging playmaker, would take the reigns. A binding agent was sorely needed.

DEADLINE DOUBLE-DOWN

With Valanciunas sidelined indefinitely and Leonard and Lowry swapping absences for rest and various maladies, the Raptors began to sputter in the weeks following the win at Oracle Arena. Some standout wins snuck onto the team's ledger — most notably a 123-116 win over the amazing Bucks sans Lowry — but concerns over chemistry lingered. During the team's 59-win campaign a year prior, the bench was a revelation. With Poeltl shipped off in the Leonard deal, Pascal Siakam undergoing a transformation to stardom as a 30-minute starter, and C.J. Miles stuck in a season-long slump, Nurse's reserves became more liability than asset. Something about the Raptors' mix was a little stinky. Not much time remained to spruce it up.

Ahead of the February 7th trade deadline,

Masai Ujiri (center) added Kawhi Leonard (left) and Danny Green (right) in a blockbuster off-season trade, giving the Raptors a true superstar in Leonard and a savvy glue guy and sharpshooter in Green.

Philadelphia's future-bombing deal to land Tobias Harris, along with the Bucks' acquisitions of George Hill and Nikola Mirotic, jacked up the pressure on Ujiri and Webster to make a move to keep pace.

Marc Gasol — the former Defensive Player of the Year and an all-time great passing centre — became a Raptor less than an hour before the 3pm buzzer. Headed to the Memphis Grizzlies were Delon Wright, Miles, and Valanciunas, the latter of whom was cruelly set to return from injury after two months away that night.

As was the case with the DeRozan trade, the deal came with an emotional toll. Valanciunas was the co-longest serving Raptor next to Lowry, and had been critical to playoff series wins over Indiana, Miami, and Washington in the past.

"A big day for us and a tough day, too," said Ujiri to assembled media on deadline day. "You build camaraderie, you build a family, and then you have to do these kind of things and it makes it difficult."

Championships aren't won without a little ruthlessness, though. Toronto's disparate halves threatened to derail the team in the most dire postseason moments. Who better to tie them together than Gasol, the ultimate connector?

"I think we added a player that's very savvy. In the playoffs you need experience. Going forward you need really strong basketball minds, toughness," said Ujiri. "You need size, you need shooting from outside, basketball IQ, everything. It combines it all."

Later than night, a shorthanded Raptors team would play its last low stakes game of the season, against the Hawks. Without Leonard or the guys involved in the deal, Siakam posted 33 points and 14 boards on just 20 shots, highlighting another reason why this year's version of the team was worth doubling-down on. Soon, Gasol would arrive and the stretch drive would begin. Ujiri's construction of the Raptors championship puzzle was complete.

DEROZAN'S RETURN

With the roster assembled and the All-Star break out of the way, the Raptors had one last bit of business to take care of before the drive for the playoffs. DeMar DeRozan's Spurs schooled the Raptors in Kawhi Leonard's return to a hostile San Antonio the month prior, but DeRozan's real closure would have to wait until February 22nd, back in Toronto.

The scene in DeRozan's old home arena could not have been more different from the one in Texas in early January. A rousing tribute video at the first timeout sent Scotiabank Arena to its feet for an ovation lasting more than a minute. It was the proper goodbye DeRozan wasn't afforded with the trade going down in the dead of summer.

All pleasantries were set aside in crunch time — the portion of games for which DeRozan faced the most scrutiny during his time with the Raptors. After a missed Serge Ibaka free throw, DeRozan walked the ball up the court, the Spurs leading 117-116 with the shot clock and game clock virtually even. What happened next laid bare all the reasons why Ujiri pulled the trigger on a deal he knew would draw scorn initially.

Leonard and Lowry converged on DeRozan at half court, and the former came away with the ball. He took it the other way for a dunk that put the Raptors up for good.

"Kyle ... know[s] how to guard me obviously," DeRozan said after the game. This underscored the ceiling-capping flaws inherent to DeRozan's game. Guarding him was easier to figure out than guarding bona fide superstars like Leonard.

With a proper reception given to DeRozan and living, on-court proof of the trade's virtue now in existence, Raptors fans could look ahead to a run to the postseason, guilt-free.

COMING TOGETHER

Nick Nurse's challenge to finish the season was to settle on the base game plan for the playoffs. Massaging the fit of his best players took top priority. After some brief flip-flopping of Gasol and Ibaka as the starting centres, an Ibaka suspension handed the gig to Gasol for good. With a limited runway to get sorted, the new starting five of Lowry, Green, Leonard, Ibaka, and Gasol made good on the immense potential of a group with such combined shooting, defensive acumen, and basketball intellect. It was a fivesome that just made sense. Outscoring opponents by 12 points every 100 possessions across 161 minutes together portended good things to come.

Health, as was the case all season, was the bugaboo. Leonard's load management days persisted until season's end. Fred VanVleet sat over a month to nurse a thumb injury that doubled as recuperation time for his achy back.

But heading into the playoffs, fans could rest easy knowing everything that could be done had been done to prepare the team for a fruitful postseason run. With 58 wins, the second-best record in the conference and league locked up, a killer starting five paced by a legitimate superstar, and a roster somewhere near full health, the Raptors were ready to cash in on Ujiri's big bet. ∎

Among the biggest off-season storylines in the NBA in 2018 were the movement of Kawhi Leonard and LeBron James. Kawhi won an NBA title, while LeBron and the Lakers missed the playoffs in the Western Conference.

Coach

NICK NURSE

Nurse's Coaching Odyssey Perfectly Prepared Him for the Moment in Toronto

By Alex Wong

The Des Moines Register's 1985 Male Athlete of the Year in high school, Nick Nurse, a native of Carroll, Iowa, attended Northern Iowa and had a standout college career as a point guard of the team, setting a handful of school records for three-point shooting. Despite the accolades and records as a high school and college player, Nurse was never destined for the NBA, at least not as a player. He earned a B.A. in accounting at Northern Iowa and set his sights on joining the coaching ranks at a young age.

After serving as a student assistant coach at Northern Iowa, Nurse, still in his early 20's at the time, received his first coaching offer: to be a player-coach for the Derby Storm of the British Basketball League. Considering his other options, including a more lucrative offer to play in Germany, he boarded a plane and headed overseas for a unique challenge.

In Derby, Nurse's age and limited coaching experience made the transition a tad bit overwhelming. He was preparing to be both the team's starting point guard and head coach. "I remember calling my high school and college coaches right away," Nurse said. "I also went and got a whole bunch of videos and books and just started making practice plans."

He didn't know it at the time, but every experience from this point on was preparing Nurse to become an NBA head coach who would be flexible, adaptable, and willing to adjust on the fly, the exact qualities the Toronto Raptors were looking for heading into the 2018-19 season after years of playoff disappointment.

The first challenge of Nurse's coaching career in the British Basketball League: he was giving out orders to players who were all at least 10 years older than him. "It was awkward," Nurse said. "The one good thing is because I was the point guard, I could control things on the floor."

It took time, but Nurse eventually found his groove and earned the respect of his teammates with his preparation and work ethic. It also helped that his resume started to grow. In nine seasons in the British Basketball League coaching four different teams, Nurse had a 276-103 record, a .728 winning percentage. He was named Coach of the Year twice and won two championships.

By 2007, his coaching journey had taken him to the NBA Development League, which was still in its early stages. Des Moines had been awarded an expansion franchise. Given a chance to return home and be one step away from being in the NBA coaching ranks, Nurse

Nick Nurse's winding journey through the coaching ranks took him around the world, culminating in Toronto with an NBA championship.

accepted an offer to coach the Iowa Energy.

Once again, Nurse needed to be malleable coaching in a league where roster turnover was the norm and players weren't exactly looking to play within a system, but often looking for their own shot in order to fill out the stat sheet for a chance to be somewhere else. "The nice way of putting it is that it was a transitionary league," Nurse said. "It's unbelievable training for rebuilding chemistry during a season. In another league, a coach will get a team, and once the chemistry is right, it stays that way. In the D-League, you're rebuilding that 10 to 15 times within a single season."

By the summer of 2013, Nurse had accomplished all that he could as a coach outside of the NBA. In his six seasons in the D-League with the Energy and later the Rio Grande Valley Vipers, Nurse finished with a 192-123 record and became the first head coach in D-League history to lead two different teams to the championship. He finally received the call-up he was waiting for in July 2013, when the Raptors hired him to join Dwane Casey's coaching staff for the 2013-14 season.

After five seasons as an assistant coach in Toronto, Nurse got his chance to step into the head coaching role when president Masai Ujiri decided to fire Coach of the Year Dwane Casey in search of a coach who he could trust to win chess matches and out-manage the opposing team's head coach over a seven-game series, something Casey had fell short of doing each postseason.

Nurse's coaching experience overseas and in the D-League served as perfect preparation for what would face Nurse during his first season as an NBA head coach with the Raptors. They needed to integrate Kawhi Leonard into the fold, while shuffling starting lineups on a nightly basis during the regular season. This was thanks to a load management plan agreed upon between Leonard and the team's medical staff

Nurse is the fifth rookie coach in the modern NBA era to win a championship in his first year, joining Tyronn Lue, his Finals counterpart Steve Kerr, Pat Riley, and Paul Westhead.

that limited him to 60 games and restricted his minutes in order to keep their star player healthy and ready for the playoffs, where he would lead all postseason players in minutes played.

A midseason trade that brought Marc Gasol to the team would shuffle the deck once again and gave Nurse a limited amount of time to put all the pieces on the roster in the right place before the start of the postseason. Certainly, the experiences in the D-League served as a blueprint for how Nurse would manage to pull the Raptors together into a cohesive unit in the playoffs, where the Raptors found their identity as an elite defensive team and followed Nurse's evolving game plan, which changed depending on matchups throughout the postseason.

Kyle Lowry admitted during the NBA Finals that Nurse yelled at the team twice all season, a remarkable feat considering the spotlight surrounding the Raptors and the urgency to integrate all the new pieces together to form a championship contending team in six months. Under the greatest pressure he had ever faced, Nurse remained the same head coach he had always been, understanding the pulse of the team and not panicking under the face of pressure.

In the journeyman head coach who spent decades toiling in obscurity, Toronto finally found the right man to lead them to the promised land. ∎

Nurse was the coaching tactician that the Raptors needed, as well as a fun personality that kept things light in the locker room.

2

Small Forward

KAWHI LEONARD

Audacious Acquisition of Leonard Pays Off in Championship Fashion for Raptors

By Alex Wong

When the San Antonio Spurs selected Kawhi Leonard with the 15th pick in the 2011 NBA Draft, they saw a physically imposing forward with massive hands and a giant wingspan who could wreak havoc on the defensive end, the kind of role player who would fit seamlessly with Tim Duncan, Tony Parker, and Manu Ginobili. What they didn't envision was that he would eventually transform and become one of the transcendent two-way superstars of our generation.

During the 2019 NBA Finals, Golden State Warriors small forward Draymond Green talked about the process of being the best at what you do. "You don't mistakenly become great," Green said. It perfectly described Leonard's rise from intriguing prospect to an NBA Finals MVP and two-time Defensive Player of the Year in San Antonio. Entering the league after two successful seasons at San Diego State, Leonard's offensive game needed polishing. His ball-handling was subpar, his playmaking lacking, his ability to break defenders off the dribble was non-existent, he didn't have a consistent jumper from the mid-range or a reliable three-point shot.

All of those things came with hard work, dedication, and plenty of hours spent in the gym. It all culminated during the 2013-14 season, when Leonard led the Spurs to an NBA championship, out-dueling LeBron James and the Miami Heat in the NBA Finals, winning the best-of-seven series 4-1, and becoming the third youngest player (22 years and 351 days) to be named NBA Finals MVP.

After Tim Duncan's retirement in 2016, Leonard was expected to carry the torch and be the face of the Spurs' franchise for the next decade. Instead, after playing in just nine games during the 2017-18 regular season while dealing with a right quadriceps injury and losing the trust of the San Antonio medical staff after disagreements over the severity of his injury and his timetable for returning to the court, Leonard requested a trade. A Southern California native, Leonard had his sights set on landing in Los Angeles, instead, he was sent to Toronto along with Danny Green in exchange for DeMar DeRozan, Jakob Poeltl, and a first round draft pick.

The trade for Kawhi Leonard sent shockwaves around the NBA and many questioned both his short and long term fit in Toronto. He answered the former in resounding fashion, leading the Raptors to a championship in his first season with the team.

After initial reports that he had no desire to report to Toronto, Leonard arrived amidst plenty of uneasiness given the circumstances of his departure from San Antonio, the Raptors not being his preferred destination, and the fact he would be a free agent in a year's time. But what the Raptors fans discovered was a no-nonsense superstar, the exact type of dominant player they had been lacking in previous playoff runs to get them over the hump.

But even in their wildest imaginations, the Raptors could not have imagined the historic playoff run Leonard would go on in his first season in Toronto, where his scoring prowess and ability to deliver in the clutch started to draw comparisons to what Michael Jordan used to do in his prime with the Chicago Bulls.

In one single playoff run, Leonard provided the Raptors fanbase with more iconic moments than the entire 24 years existence of the franchise before his arrival. In the second round against the Philadelphia 76ers, Leonard had the ball in his hands in Game 7 with the game tied and just seconds left on the clock. He dribbled from one side of the court to the other, finding just enough space to rise up over the outstretched hands of Joel Embiid. As he crouched near the Raptors bench on the follow through, the ball bounced on the rim four times as an entire country held its breath. In a few seconds, the season and a franchise that took a chance on a superstar that could take them to places they had never been before watched helplessly. Finally, the ball fell through the rim.

Leonard let out a scream as the home crowd at Scotiabank Arena went berserk. Outside, thousands of fans who gathered at the outdoor screening area named Jurassic Park took to the streets to celebrate. Leonard and the city of Toronto were finally tied together by an iconic moment, the first of its kind. It was the first Game 7 buzzer beating series clincher in NBA playoff history.

Even while battling leg injuries in the Eastern Conference Finals, Leonard took his game to the next level, seen here finishing resoundingly over Milwaukee's Giannis Antetokounmpo.

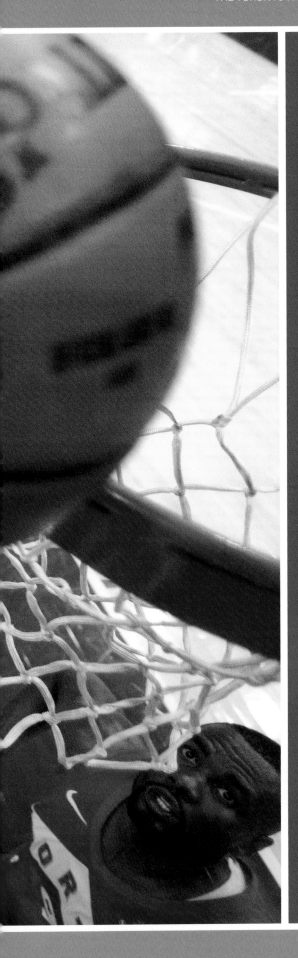

As the playoffs progressed, Leonard grew to appreciate the city of Toronto and a fanbase that expanded beyond not just the city, but to the entire country of Canada. They painted murals of him in downtown Toronto, celebrated him as a folk hero, and he started to notice.

"I appreciate them for their support," Leonard told reporters during the 2019 NBA Finals. "Coming in, I wanted to be able to contribute to the team and be able to get them to this point. I just feel like I did something special for them."

Leonard did more for the Raptors fanbase that he could ever imagine, erasing years of doubt and feelings of inferiority, turning a hockey town into a city that would set television ratings records over and over again during their playoff run, as an entire nation rallied behind the basketball team up north that kept surprising all of their doubters.

In the process, Leonard left a legacy behind in Toronto that they will talk about for generations, and he did so with the same approach that he always had: a laser focus on being the best teammate and the best team, and not chasing any individual accolades or the fame that comes with being one of the best players in the world.

"I'm not playing the game for that reason," Leonard told reporters during the NBA Finals. "I'm out here playing to have fun and trying to be the best player I can be. I'm happy with myself and what I've done in my career. It's not about me being famous or wanting to have more fame than those guys. It's about me playing basketball and having fun on the floor." ■

The load management strategy employed by Leonard and the Raptors paid off in the playoffs, as he dominated his opponents throughout, culminating in the first championship in team history.

7

Point Guard

KYLE LOWRY

Lowry's Perseverance is Rewarded with a Long-Awaited NBA Title

By Alex Wong

The 2013-14 season was the start of the *We The North* era for the Toronto Raptors. Toronto appeared on their way to a sixth straight season of missing the playoffs. Masai Uijri seemed intent on starting a full-on rebuild for the franchise, and tanking for better odds in the NBA Draft lottery looked like the primary goal. In December, the Raptors were below .500 and had just traded Rudy Gay to the Sacramento Kings. Kyle Lowry was next on the trading block.

A proposed deal with the New York Knicks was near completion, to the point where Lowry had his bags packed in his Toronto home, ready to head to the airport for his next destination. In the last minute, the Knicks decided to pull out of the deal, and so the greatest six-year run in Raptors franchise history was accidentally launched, with Lowry becoming the heart and soul of the franchise.

In the same season, alongside DeMar DeRozan, Lowry helped lead the Raptors back to the playoffs.

A competitive series in the first round against the Brooklyn Nets ended as Lowry's game-winning attempt was blocked at the buzzer in Game 7 at home. Toronto would come back each season vowing to change their postseason fortunes, and finally broke through in 2016 and advanced to the Eastern Conference Finals, but lost to the Cleveland Cavaliers in six games, starting a streak of three consecutive playoffs where Toronto would run into LeBron James and be eliminated.

After a second straight sweep at the hands of James and the Cavs last season, DeMar DeRozan was traded to San Antonio and Dwane Casey was fired, replaced by Nick Nurse. A midseason trade of Jonas Valanciunas meant Lowry was the only remaining member of the 2013-14 team left on the roster.

The 2018-19 season was a difficult one for Lowry. He started out strong and was among the league leaders in assists but did not appear happy with the organization for trading his best friend in DeRozan. In an early season interview with Rachel Nichols of ESPN, he

Kyle Lowry's patience as the longest-tenured member of the Raptors paid off with a NBA title in 2019.

expressed his displeasure with short and curt responses about his relationship with Ujiri, saying he was the player and Ujiri was the general manager, leaving room for interpretation as to his discontent.

After his interview, Lowry went into a shooting slump, and before the trade deadline, rumors were swirling that he would be dealt. Lowry sat down with Ujiri and finally had the conversation they needed to get on the right page, and they set their differences aside in order to help pursue a common goal: winning a championship.

If DeRozan was the face of the franchise, and the first player to truly declare his loyalty to the city of Toronto, Lowry was the behind-the-scenes engine that made everything go. Players around the locker room have always said: as Lowry goes, so do the Raptors.

His contributions don't always show up on the stat sheet, because most of what Lowry does is simply winning plays, whether it is deflections on the defensive end, putting teammates in the right position to succeed on the offensive end by threading passes in just the right spots, sacrificing his own body by drawing defensive charges against larger more imposing players in the lane, or defending opposing big men in the low post with ease. Lowry has always been the player that makes the Raptors go, even on nights when he's not scoring the basketball.

Playing alongside a superstar of Kawhi Leonard's caliber required an in-season adjustment from Lowry, to move away from a primary scoring role he had been asked of on previous Raptors team, but instead be the point guard to help integrate many new pieces into the team, while shifting into a complimentary role on the offensive end.

For other players, it would seem like the shift in role would have felt like a demotion, but for Lowry, it has always been about the greater goals, to get to the NBA Finals and win a championship, to validate all of the years he has spent working to become one of the best point guards in the NBA, even if he is rarely mentioned with the more popular guards around the league.

In a postseason filled with memorable moments, perhaps the best one for Lowry came after the Raptors clinched the Eastern Conference championship on their home floor. As they gathered on a podium at center court to receive their trophy, Lowry received an even larger standing ovation than Leonard, as the home crowd chanted his name and showed their appreciation for the one player who has been here for the longest. The usually business-like Lowry couldn't help but break into a smile and chuckle to himself at that exact moment.

"It means a lot," Lowry told reporters afterwards. "It's taken a long time to get here in my career." ■

Lowry's time in Toronto has been occasionally tumultuous — he's almost been traded, and he was frustrated to see he best friend DeMar DeRozan sent packing — but he stuck it out and earned a championship as a result.

OVERLOOKED NO MORE

Fred VanVleet, Norman Powell, and Pascal Siakam Are an Improbable Championship Trio

By Alex Wong

When Toronto Raptors guard Fred VanVleet first came into the league, he wondered whether opposing players even knew who he was. "People were probably like who … is this kid, coming into the game, picking us up full court," VanVleet said. "I don't look like an NBA player to most guys."

The 25-year-old guard is just one of many players on the 2018-19 roster who have their own underdog story. Undrafted after four years at Wichita State, VanVleet starred for the Raptors' summer league team before signing a contract with the team and earning an invite to training camp, where he beat out several other players for a spot on the final roster.

In his second season, VanVleet finished third in Sixth Man of the Year voting and became one of the most reliable bench scorers in the entire league. In the Eastern Conference Finals, it was VanVleet's 14-for-17 shooting from beyond the arc in the final three games against the Milwaukee Bucks (all victories for Toronto) that helped send them to the NBA finals.

VanVleet isn't the only person in the locker room who's had to prove himself to earn a spot on an NBA roster. His closest friend on the team, Norman Powell, was taken 46th in the second round in 2015. Many believed he was too undersized and without an elite set of skills to make it in the league. Instead, in each of his first four seasons in the league, Powell played a starring role in postseason wins which helped rescue the Raptors' playoff chances.

"I was overlooked," Powell said. "There were all these different variables about my game that made people think I wouldn't be a good player in the league."

VanVleet and Powell's stories are inspiring, but perhaps none feels more improbable than Pascal Siakam, who was taken 27th overall in the 2016 by the Toronto Raptors. On draft night, there wasn't any buzz about the selection. Siakam, who didn't start playing basketball until he was 16, was viewed as an athletic talent but very raw when it came to understanding the game. But each season Siakam would improve, adding new moves to his increasingly lethal arsenal on the offensive end and would start thinking the game better too, turning himself into one of the best defenders in the NBA.

During the 2018-19 season, Siakam broke through and became one of the rising stars in the league, playing a starring role alongside Kawhi Leonard on a championship team. He was named one of the candidates for the Most Improved Player award. During Toronto's postseason run, Siakam went up against

Norman Powell has overcome doubts about whether he belonged in the NBA to become a key offensive spark off the bench for the Raptors.

some of the best defenders in the league, including Joel Embiid, Giannis Antetokounmpo, and Draymond Green, and continued to hold his own. While he showed the ups and downs that most young players go through in their first extended playoff run, Siakam would always figure things out or find new ways to attack opposing defenses, showing glimpses of a potential franchise player in the making.

The makeup of any championship team requires a superstar to lead the way, but the supporting cast can play a huge role too. The Raptors were the first team to play in the NBA Finals without a lottery pick on their roster in league history, and leading the way were Siakam, VanVleet, and Powell, all of whom played a huge role at different points in the postseason run.

Their success speaks to not only their belief and work ethic, but also the Raptors organization and their focus on player development. All three players spent time in the G-League (Siakam won a Most Valuable Player award there) and the time they put in with Toronto's coaching staff saw them go from promising prospects to key cogs on a championship team.

The fact Toronto was the first championship team without a lottery pick may seem like an anomaly, but in fact it might highlight one of the strengths of this franchise: playing in a market where A-list free agents have never considered as a potential destination, the development of homegrown talent is so imperative to helping the franchise find an edge. In this category, Toronto exceeded everyone's expectations, and in the process, planted the seeds for a championship contender in their own backyard. ∎

Fred VanVleet (left) and Pascal Siakam (right) entered the NBA inconspicuously, yet have gone on to thrive in their respective roles — bench scoring extraordinaire for VanVleet and budding superstar for Siakam.

President of Basketball Operations

MASAI UJIRI

Ujiri Put Onus on Himself to Guide Raptors to Championship Heights

By Alex Wong

After the Toronto Raptors were swept last season by the Cleveland Cavaliers in the second round of the playoffs, putting a disappointing end to a season where they set a franchise record for regular season wins (59), team president Masai Ujiri fired the eventual Coach of the Year Dwane Casey and traded away DeMar DeRozan, the face of the franchise who spoke regularly about spending his entire career in Toronto.

"Put it on me," Ujiri told reporters shortly after his team was eliminated by LeBron James and the Cavaliers for a third consecutive season, the last two via sweeps. The president of the team put the onus on himself to put the team over the top.

Ujiri has always believed in the Raptors and in the city of Toronto more than the fanbase has sometimes been willing to reciprocate. He has spoken and carried himself like the president of a team with championship aspirations, but after five consecutive postseason trips, three of which ended in embarrassing sweeps, it was time for a change.

Having taken a franchise toiling in mediocrity and turned it into a perennial playoff contender wasn't enough for Ujiri, he only wanted to chase the ultimate goal: bringing a championship north of the border and validating the Raptors as one of the top-flight franchises in the NBA.

To do so, Ujiri took two major risks. In replacing Casey, he went with journeyman coach Nick Nurse, who would be tasked with guiding the Raptors to a championship as a rookie NBA head coach. Ujiri also traded DeRozan to the San Antonio Spurs in exchange for Kawhi Leonard, even with questions surrounding his health, his impending free agency, and whether he had any desire to be in Toronto.

After initial reports surfaced that he would not report to Toronto at all, Leonard ended up wearing a Raptors uniform on media day in September, walking in with teammate Danny Green and Ujiri to the podium for one of the most highly anticipated press conferences in franchise history.

There was a nervous energy in the air, as the

Masai Ujiri managed to continuously tweak the Raptors' roster over the years, avoiding any large-scale rebuild and keeping the team consistently competitive until breaking through for a championship in 2019.

Raptors were about to embark on a one-year journey filled with uncertainty. Ujiri was, literally and figuratively, under the spotlight in this very moment, and he took the opportunity to set the tone for the entire 2018-19 season.

"The narrative of not wanting to come to this city is gone," Ujiri told reporters passionately after being tossed several questions about Leonard's uncertain future in Toronto. "I think that's old and we should move past that. Believe in this city, believe in yourself. We can stop talking about coming to the city or wanting to come to the city that's old talk. We want to win. We have a privilege and an opportunity to be one of the NBA teams here. That's a huge privilege for us and it's our jobs here to try and get these players. It's our jobs to try and sell it to these players here, but we're proud of who we are, we're proud to have these guys. We're proud to have the young guys we have. We're proud of what Kyle Lowry and everybody has done here. So let's move past that narrative of wanting to stay here or wanting to come here."

In return, the 2018-19 Raptors validated all of Ujiri's moves. Leonard's historic playoff run means Toronto has already won the trade, regardless of whether he returns next season. In Nurse, the Raptors finally had a head coach who was adaptable and malleable in the postseason, and willing to be assertive in making adjustments and thinking several steps ahead, with the mindset of putting players in a position to succeed.

It wasn't just the hiring of Nurse and the acquisition of Leonard. At the trade deadline, the Raptors felt like they were still one piece away from putting together a championship contending starting five. Even with Serge Ibaka's finest season yet in Toronto, the Raptors knew they needed one more player to slot into the starting

unit in order to create the connectivity required on both ends of the floor. After exploring several trade options around the league, Ujiri traded several pieces including Jonas Valanciunas in exchange for centre Marc Gasol, a former Defensive Player of the Year.

The move solidified the Raptors heading into the playoffs. Gasol was a fulcrum on offense, often working as a second point guard on the floor, facilitating at the top of the key, and helping turn Toronto into the best three-point shooting team in the regular season after his arrival, thanks to his ball movement and willingness to spot the open man.

On defense, Gasol proved valuable during the playoff run, helping to contain All-Star centres including Nikola Vucevic and Joel Embiid. The Raptors wouldn't be where they are without the Kawhi Leonard trade, but the Marc Gasol trade was arguably just as important.

In finally pushing his chips all-in, Ujiri was validated for not standing pat and waiting another year for playoff disappointment to unfold. He was aggressive, assertive, and made all the right moves. In the end, he was rewarded for all of them. ∎

Ujiri's trade for Kawhi Leonard (left) and Danny Green (right) is rightfully lauded as the move that truly put the Raptors on a championship level, but his hiring of Nick Nurse and acquisition of Marc Gasol were also essential in elevating the franchise to unparalleled heights in team history.

BACK WHERE THEY BELONG

Serge Ibaka and Marc Gasol Are Teammates Again and Appreciative of Their Journey to the Finals

By Alex Wong

Seven years ago, as the clock ticked down on the final seconds of Game 5 of the 2012 NBA Finals and the Miami Heat wrapped up a 4-1 series win over the Oklahoma City Thunder, Serge Ibaka and the rest of his teammates — which included three future NBA MVPs in Kevin Durant, Russell Westbrook, and James Harden — were certain they would return. Everyone believed the Thunder were primed to dominate the next decade but just months later, Harden was traded to Houston. Durant eventually left for Golden State. Ibaka was traded to Orlando the same summer.

Seven years later, as the clock ticked down on the final seconds of Game 6 of the 2019 Eastern Conference Finals at Scotiabank Arena, Ibaka hugged his teammates, smiled through the entire post-game celebration, and even sang a song in the locker room to celebrate his return to the NBA Finals. In between, he's gone from Oklahoma City, to Orlando, to Toronto, and became the forgotten member of the core four that started with the Thunder. He's also grown to appreciate a second opportunity in the Finals.

"Man, after seven years, it seemed like most people thought it was over for me," said Ibaka days before the start of the NBA Finals. "But I always believed. I always put in the work. A lot of guys in the league have never seen the NBA Finals. This is my second time. I am so thankful."

The journey was just as arduous for Marc Gasol, who finally made his first NBA Finals appearance in his 11th season in the league. Before he was acquired by the Raptors at the trade deadline, Gasol had spent his entire career with the Memphis Grizzlies and was part of the foundation that helped build the Grit N' Grind identity in Memphis, a hard-nosed basketball team who always made themselves a difficult opponent in the postseason. Even when other teams had more talent, the Grizzlies would push back with their cohesion and physical play.

Gasol is a three-time All-Star, a Defensive Player of the Year, and was named to the All-NBA First Team in 2015, but after he was selected 48th overall by the Los Angeles Lakers in 2008, he was traded the following season to Memphis and viewed as a throw-in player in a trade that helped the Lakers acquire his older brother Pau Gasol, leading to two championships in Los Angeles.

The mid-season deal to acquire Gasol also pushed Ibaka into a bench role. It was made easier by the fact that Gasol and Ibaka are teammates on the Spanish national team, but also because Ibaka realizes, after taking his own long and winding road back to the Finals, just how important it is to give up some of your individual goals for the betterment of the team.

"The sacrifices were not easy," Ibaka said. "But you make those sacrifices and you say everything is about

Serge Ibaka was moved into a bench role after the acquisition of Marc Gasol, an adjustment that he took in stride for the greater good of the team.

the team. Now the sacrifices are paying off. It's not about my performance. It's about the team winning. I was disappointed last year because the team lost. Last playoff, I had a couple of great games, but the team lost, and that was disappointing."

Ibaka and Gasol could not be any different. On the court, Ibaka is the energizer, whose rim protection and blocked shots can electrify a crowd. He can also do something similar on the offensive end with his rim-rocking dunks. Gasol is the more cerebral of the two, picking apart opposing defenses with his ability to see a play unfold before it actually happens. Together, the two Spanish national team teammates gave the Raptors a centre tandem that gave head coach Nick Nurse the flexibility to match up against opposing teams and their tendencies, whether it was against larger lineups by utilizing Gasol's size, or smaller lineups by employing Ibaka's ability to run out in transition and defend smaller players at the five position.

Ibaka and Gasol's ability to share their minutes and understand that on any given night, one of them might be spending most of crunch time on the bench, spoke to the selfless attitude that permeated this team during their postseason run.

"This is a special group," Ibaka said. "Very special. Our togetherness. Everybody really cares about the team. You don't really have guys with egos here. Even guys who don't play, you see them cheering for the team, that's good. When things go wrong, we don't point fingers. We talk, we watch film and get better." ∎

Serge Ibaka and Marc Gasol are also teammates on the Spanish national team, adding a layer of chemistry and familiarity to the Raptors and helping in the roster transition.

14
Shooting Guard

DANNY GREEN

Green's Winding Journey to the NBA Helped Make Him the Ideal Championship Glue Guy

By Alex Wong

Inside a P.F. Chang's in Boise, Idaho in early 2011, Danny Green sat down with Jeremy Lin and Steve Novak, teammates on the Reno Bighorns of the NBA Development League to chat about their basketball careers. Green would eventually become a championship role player in the NBA, but at that moment he was hanging on to a professional basketball career that felt like it was slipping away.

After a successful college career at North Carolina, Green joined the Cleveland Cavaliers and played 20 games as a rookie before he was waived. The San Antonio Spurs picked him up, but Green was released after appearing in just two games in November. Without an NBA team interested in his services, Green spent Thanksgiving and Christmas at home with his family and contemplated playing overseas in Italy, before his agent convinced him the best route back in the league would be to join the D-League.

The experience with the Reno Bighorns was humbling. When Green signed with the team, he didn't even know where he was, perhaps symbolic given how lost he was in his basketball career. "I didn't

know geography well," Green said. "I was thinking, Reno is in Nevada, it's gotta be close to Las Vegas. Instead, it was far … The total opposite, and it was cold ..." He also found life as a development league player to be much different. "They spoil you so much in the NBA," Green said. "… But really, it wasn't that bad. It was just normal life."

Normal life meant taking the team van to get his own groceries, cooking breakfast for himself in the morning, and scrambling before games to find a trainer who would tape him up. One thing did work in Green's favour: because there was an odd number of players on the team, he would luck out and get his own hotel room sometimes on road trips instead of having to share with a teammate.

Green also got lucky with the head coach of the team, Eric Musselman, who saw his potential on the offensive end and made him the team's primary scoring threat. After a short stint in Reno, the Spurs came calling again, and this time, Green would not only stick with the team, but eventually set an NBA Finals record for three-pointers made, turning himself into one of

Since arriving in Toronto, Danny Green has brought championship experience and essential leadership to this Raptors squad.

the best three-and-D players in the league, winning a championship in 2014, and being named to the NBA All-Defensive Second Team in 2017.

Green's arrival in Toronto did not receive the same amount of anticipation and buzz as Kawhi Leonard, but he became just as valuable to the team's goal of winning a championship. During the regular season, Green was one of the most reliable and durable players on the roster, starting 80 games and shooting 45.5 percent from three, second in the league behind Joe Harris of the Brooklyn Nets.

Early in the season, Green saw the potential of this Raptors team as it was starting to come together. "I think we have something special here in Toronto with the core group," Green said. "If we can keep everybody together and continue to grow, I think we can change the organization around to being something different."

A lot of that change was thanks to Green himself and the championship experience and calming influence which he brought both to the locker room and on the floor. It was the kind of veteran leadership which the Raptors sought and needed, a player who could hit a big shot to stem an opposing team's run and could also make an impact on the defensive end.

While Raptors fans waited for any inkling of Leonard being intrigued by the prospects of staying long term in Toronto, Green was quick to embrace the organization and the city. "I love this organization," Green said during the season. "I love this group that we have — a very talented group. The coaching staff is a lot of fun to play for and the fans, you can't beat it."

Every championship team needs a glue guy, someone who is never fazed, who will not let a shooting slump affect their play on the defensive end, a solid supporting player who is never afraid of the moment. Without these players, a superstar can only lead a team by himself so far. In Danny Green, the Raptors found just the right player that checked the boxes for every quality they have been looking for from a wing player that they desperately needed for years to turn them into a championship team. ∎

Danny Green is shadowed by Boston Celtics guard Kyrie Irving during a February game in Toronto, a city which Green has thoroughly embraced.

EASTERN CONFERENCE QUARTER NALS, GAME I

Magic 104, Raptors 101
April 13, 2019 · Toronto, Ontario

ZAPPED

Game 1 Struggles Continue, Raptors Drop Opener at Home

By Alex Wong

After a successful regular season in which the Raptors finished with 58 wins and the number two seed in the Eastern Conference, a first round matchup with the Orlando Magic wasn't supposed to be a challenge. Everyone expected the Raptors, with a veteran starting lineup loaded with playoff experience, to move on relatively easily to the second round. Or so we thought.

Past Raptors teams have entered the postseason with high expectations only to run into a wall. More importantly, Toronto has struggled so much in opening games of playoff series it has become a running joke that every series involving the Raptors should just start with them trailing 1-0 in Game 2.

This year was supposed to be different. The Raptors had Kawhi Leonard, a superstar player with an NBA Finals MVP on his resume. They also have an experienced group around him, who weren't going to wilt under the bright lights. If there was one concern heading into the playoffs, it was that thanks to the load management of Leonard during the regular season which limited him to 60 games, and the mid-season trade for Marc Gasol, the constant shuffling of rotations during the regular season didn't give the core group a significant amount of time to familiarize themselves with each other on the court.

The lack of familiarity would end up being the difference in Game 1 against the Magic at home. After racing out to a five-point lead after the first quarter, the Raptors allowed Orlando to score 32 points in the second period. Leading 42-41 with under four minutes left in the half, the Magic went on a 15-0 run to extend their lead to 16 points before settling for an eight-point lead at halftime.

The young Magic team seemed unfazed despite being underdogs on the road. Aaron Gordon had a double-double with 10 points and 10 rebounds. Evan Fournier scored 16 points. Jonathan Isaac added 11 points.

The Raptors' one-two punch of Leonard and Pascal Siakam delivered, with 25 and 24 points respectively and helped lead a second half comeback. With under two minutes remaining in the fourth quarter, Leonard tied the game with a three-pointer and then hit a go-ahead jumper with a minute remaining. After D.J. Augustin evened the score at 101 apiece, the Magic got the ball back with a chance to pull off a Game 1 upset on the road.

In the biggest possession of the game, a lack of communication between two former Defensive Players of the Year would befall the Raptors. As Augustin attacked Toronto's defense, Leonard and Gasol weren't decisive enough with their defensive rotations. In that split second, it allowed enough space for Augustin to make the game-winning three-pointer, sending the Magic to a 104-101 victory, and a surprising 1-0 series lead. Augustin finished with 25 points in 30 minutes.

"It was a mistake made on that play," Gasol admitted afterwards. "We miscommunicated and he made a good shot."

The final play not only brought back memories of past playoff failures and dropped Toronto's franchise

Raptors centre Marc Gasol dives for the ball as Magic guard D.J. Augustin leaps out of the way during the first half. Augustin would go on to make the game-winning shot following a defensive misstep by Gasol.

record in Game 1s to an appalling 2-14, but it was also a disappointing start to the postseason for Kyle Lowry, who went scoreless in 34 minutes finishing 0-for-7 from the field and 0-for-6 from beyond the arc.

After working all season for home court advantage and talking about the regular season as an 82-game practice for the playoff run, it was an ominous start for a group with championship aspirations. But there was no panic in the locker room afterwards.

"It's first one to win four games," Gasol said. "You go back, watch film, see what worked, see what didn't work, see what you've got to be better at and play the next game."

The consensus heading into the playoffs was the Eastern Conference comprised of four contenders: Toronto, Milwaukee, Boston, and Philadelphia and that

the first round would be a cakewalk for all of the favorites.

Instead, Orlando showed up to Toronto, where the Raptors finished 32-9 at Scotiabank Arena, and stole Game 1. The Raptors knew their path to a championship wasn't going to be easy, not with the talent makeup of the top teams in the East, but they certainly weren't expecting the first crisis point of their postseason run to come just one game in.

But it certainly seemed fitting for the Raptors to open their most anticipated playoff run with a home loss. This is a franchise that has never made anything easy, that have created an aura of playoff anxiety around the fanbase that has become hard to shake. All of this would be tested again.

One game into the postseason, the Raptors were forced to go back to the drawing board and regroup. ∎

Raptors 111, Magic 82
April 16, 2019 • Toronto, Ontario

BACK ON TRACK

Raptors Even Series in Game 2 with Complete Performance

By Alex Wong

After a disappointing Game 1 loss, all eyes were on Kyle Lowry and the Raptors to respond in Game 2, and they didn't disappoint. Just over a minute into the first quarter, Lowry, coming off a scoreless performance in Game 1, split a pair of free throws, receiving a thunderous response from the home crowd. Lowry rebounded and finished with 22 points on 8-for-13 shooting and added seven assists.

This time around, it was the Magic who had to deal with their own scoring drought. The Raptors dialed up their defensive intensity in Game 2, holding the Magic scoreless for the first five minutes of the game, forcing them into six missed shots from the field. Orlando didn't help their own cause, missing four straight free throws during that span. By the time they finally managed to get a basket, the Raptors had raced out to an 11-0 lead. Toronto ended the first half with a 51-39 lead, holding Orlando to 33 percent shooting from the floor.

After shaking off an early playoff slump, Lowry ceded the spotlight to Kawhi Leonard in the second half. In a 39-point third quarter, Leonard put on a show for the home crowd, scoring 17 points on 7-of-9 shooting to open up a 90-66 lead heading into the fourth quarter.

Leonard finished with 37 points on 15-for-22 shooting and set a career playoff-high in field goals made. By the time he checked out for the final time with the Raptors up by 31 points late in the fourth quarter,

he received a standing ovation from the home crowd, who had waited all season to see their superstar fully unleashed. After a Game 1 loss, they got their wish and the Raptors coasted to a 111-82 victory to even the best-of-seven series at 1-1.

Despite leading the way, Leonard was happy to credit his point guard for his Game 2 performance. "He did a great job of bouncing back," Leonard told reporters after the game. "He's a pro. That's what pros do, they know it's just one game and they come in the next game ready to play."

His head coach agreed. "He was big time tonight," Nurse said of his point guard afterwards. "That's him at his finest."

Lowry reciprocated Leonard's kind words with some of his own. "Tonight he was just in a groove, getting downhill, getting to his spots," Lowry said. "He's a player who knows where he wants to be on the floor and when he gets to those spots, he's pretty tough to guard."

"Leonard was great," Magic head coach Steve Clifford said after the Game 2 loss. "What are you going to do? He was great."

The game provided a first glimpse at what a successful playoff blueprint would look like for this Raptors team. On the defensive end, they held the Magic to under 40 percent shooting from the field and 26.5 percent from three, while forcing 17 turnovers. Defense travels in the postseason, and Toronto has enough stout

Kawhi Leonard had a banner night, finishing with 37 points and logging a career playoff-high in field goals made.

individual defenders to force opposing teams into these shooting percentages on a consistent basis.

On the offensive end, the Raptors had Leonard be the dominant offensive force that he showed glimpses of during the regular season, Lowry as their engine, and Pascal Siakam as a secondary scoring option with his athleticism and ability to attack the basket. Siakam finished with 19 points on 8-for-16 shooting.

The Raptors also took care of the ball, recording just seven turnovers, and limited D.J. Augustin, who scored 25 points in a Game 1 win, to nine points and one field goal made in 23 minutes. Toronto also set a franchise record with their 29-point margin of victory.

Toronto would have preferred to win both games at home to open this series, but after another disappointing start to the playoffs, they put together a complete performance in Game 2 to make sure they wouldn't start the postseason in a 2-0 deficit. Now, it was off to Orlando for the next two games and a chance to take control of the series. ■

Raptors 98, Magic 93
April 19, 2019 • Orlando, Florida

SPOIL SPORTS

Raptors Ruin Orlando's First Home Playoff Game in Seven Years, Take Series Lead

By Alex Wong

Before tip-off, the crowd in Orlando was ready for the team's first playoff home game since 2012. Among the former Magic players in attendance included Tracy McGrady, Jameer Nelson, and Horace Grant. But once the game began, it looked like more of the same from Toronto's dominant Game 2 win.

The Raptors once again raced out to an early lead, scoring the first 10 points of the game before Orlando finally got on the board. The Magic kept fighting back in the first half and cut Toronto's lead by three points at halftime, thanks to a half court buzzer beater from Terrence Ross.

In the second half, the Raptors' new star player took over. Pascal Siakam exploded with a playoff career-high 30 points, shooting 13-for-20 from the floor, 3-of-4 from three, and adding 11 rebounds, and four assists without a turnover, while playing a team-high 42 minutes and recording a game-best plus-14 while he was on the floor.

On a night where Kawhi Leonard battled an illness that limited him to 16 points and 10 rebounds, Siakam stepped into the primary scoring role. In his first season as a full-time starter, the Most Improved Player candidate did not disappoint.

"It's just taking what a defense gives us and going with it," Siakam said afterwards.

"He's unbelievable," Kyle Lowry told reporters afterwards. "He's the most improved basketball player in the NBA this year. He's going to continue to grow and get better."

Thanks to his career night, the Raptors opened up a 17-point lead midway through the fourth quarter and appeared to be on their way to a relatively comfortable road win. A Siakam basket with 4:44 remaining put Toronto up by 12, and appeared to have snuffed out Orlando's last push, but the Magic weren't going to let their home fans down on this night, at least not without a full 48-minute effort.

Led by Ross's team-high 24 points, and 22 points and 14 rebounds from All-Star centre Nikola Vucevic, the Magic kept pushing, and pulled within three with 42 seconds left after a Ross three-pointer. Toronto had one more offensive possession to put the game away, and it was time for their point guard to come up huge.

The knock on Lowry's playoff resume has always been his up-and-down shooting, but what is often neglected is the little things the Toronto point guard does that don't show up in the box score or make highlight packages on social media and on SportsCenter. Whether it's diving for loose balls, finding open teammates, making the right reads on defense, drawing charges, or defending larger players in the low post, Lowry is a winning player. On this team, with Leonard and Siakam as scoring options, Lowry is able to play a secondary role that is more suited to his overall skillset.

Winning players have a knack for being in the right place at the right time, and that was the case for Lowry at the end of Game 3. With the Raptors up three with seconds left in the game, Lowry snuck in behind the Magic front court to steal an offensive rebound which

Pascal Siakam took the lead for the Raptors in Game 3, scoring 30 points with 11 rebounds in 42 minutes of play.

led to a pair of free throws by Leonard with 12.9 seconds remaining in the game to put the Raptors up five. Toronto would hold up for a 98-93 victory on the road to take a 2-1 series lead and regain home court advantage.

Lowry finished with 12 points and 10 rebounds, and despite Siakam's career night and Leonard's valiant performance, all teammates wanted to talk about afterwards was Lowry's key rebound.

"That rebound, talk about that rebound, that was the game," Marc Gasol said in the locker room afterwards.

"That was Kyle. That has nothing to do with scoring. He stuck his nose in there. He ran through that ball and got the rebound and won the game for us. It's a team thing. Basketball is a beautiful thing because it is a team sport and everyone has each other's back."

"It was really big," Leonard added. "Like I said before, he plays the game well. He's smart, he's going to knock down his shot, he's going to make a defensive play, he's going to set us up right on the offensive end. That's what you want from your point guard." ∎

Raptors 107, Magic 85
April 21, 2019 • Orlando, Florida

SUPERSTAR TREATMENT

Kawhi Leonard Dominates Game 4 as Raptors Take Hold of Series

By Alex Wong

When the Raptors acquired Kawhi Leonard in a trade last offseason, this was what they envisioned: a dominant superstar who could tilt the advantage to the Raptors in any best-of-seven series. In Game 4, Toronto had an opportunity to take a commanding 3-1 lead on the road, and they took care of business in convincing fashion, forcing the Orlando Magic into 17 turnovers with another impressive defensive performance. They also followed Leonard's lead on the offensive end, where the Raptors superstar scored a game-high 34 points in 35 minutes, shooting 12-for-20 from the floor, 2-for-6 from three, and adding six rebounds, two assists, two steals, and two blocks.

The Raptors led by 16 points at the half, thanks to 18 first half points from Leonard and 12 points from Pascal Siakam. In the third quarter, Leonard repeatedly answered any push from the Magic. Even though Aaron Gordon scored 16 points and made all six of his field goals in the quarter, Leonard kept pace with 12 points in the period and kept Toronto ahead 82-70 heading into the fourth quarter.

In Game 3, the Raptors had to weather a late fourth quarter run from the Magic. This time, they discovered a killer instinct in the final 12 minutes, opening the quarter with a 14-5 run, pushing the lead to 21 points and coasting to a 107-85 victory. It was the first time in Raptors franchise history in which they held a 3-1 lead in a best-of-seven series.

It was a complete performance from Leonard, who played just nine games last season with the San Antonio Spurs due to injuries, and admitted it was hard to not only be away from the floor but have to watch the playoffs instead of competing in them.

"You just want to be out there on the floor, with your teammates and just feel that team spirit and chemistry, just trying to focus on one goal," Leonard said after the game. "That's something I was missing, just being out, sitting out. That's why it's a blessing this year just to be able to play and be on the floor, regardless of what the outcome is."

"He's the Finals MVP," Gordon said. "He's doing what he's supposed to do. That's what they pay the man for, to come down here and be Kawhi Leonard."

Nick Nurse was more impressed by how the Raptors didn't let the Magic get back into the game and took advantage of an opportunity to take control of this series.

"These series, and the games in the series, are a lot about imposing your will on a team," Nurse said.

"Road wins are the best, especially in the playoffs," Leonard said.

The Raptors also got contributions from the rest of the team. Serge Ibaka scored 13 points, Kyle Lowry handed out nine assists, and Norman Powell came off the bench to score 16 points on 7-of-9 shooting.

"I feel like my teammates had a big part in tonight's win," Leonard said. "With Norm playing great, Pascal shooting the ball well, Kyle did great, made big shots, Danny [Green] made a big shot at the end of the third. Marc [Gasol] played great. Fred [VanVleet] came in and

Kawhi Leonard drives to the basket against Aaron Gordon during the first half of Game 4 in Orlando. Leonard contributed 35 points in what was a complete team effort for the Raptors.

knocked down shots. I feel like we all played well tonight, we all had our hands on the game. Once you make shots, everyone is looking at you, saying, 'You had control of the game.' You can do it on both ends of the floor and it's everybody. It's not just me out there."

Even with Leonard leading the way, the Raptors locker room realizes they will need everyone to get to where they want to go in the postseason. "We need them every night," Lowry said of the bench after the game. "If we can get that every night, it's a must for us. Those guys are so talented that they can help us in that capacity, it's great. Kawhi has a big night like tonight, it's a super bonus, but we need everyone to play their best basketball."

The defensive miscommunication that cost this team the first game of the series feels like a long time ago. After three consecutive wins, the Raptors are starting to realize they might have something special.

"I think we just go out there and play five-out basketball," Siakam said. "We have high IQ guys that can make plays. We just play off of each other. There's not a lot of play calling or things like that. We just play off of each other. It's just fun when you have guys that can understand the game with you out there." ∎

Raptors 115, Magic 96
April 23, 2019 • Toronto, Ontario

DISMISSED

Raptors Put Away Magic in First Round, Look Ahead to 76ers

By Alex Wong

By the time Kawhi Leonard checked out of Game 5 with 8:05 left to play in the fourth quarter, the Raptors were up 30 points and the home crowd at Scotiabank Arena rightfully serenaded Leonard with MVP chants.

With a chance to clinch the first round series at home, Leonard scored 27 points on just 11 field goals, finishing 8-for-11 from the field, hitting all five three pointers, while adding seven rebounds. He was a team-high plus-38 on the floor in 32 minutes, leaving no doubt who the best player and the best team was in this series.

The Raptors led by as many as 37 points in Game 5, the largest margin in a playoff game in franchise history, and coasted to a 115-96 victory, winning four consecutive games in the postseason for the first time in the team's history, and sending the Magic home with a 4-1 series win.

The script played out just the same in Game 5 as the previous three victories. Leonard led the way, but he received plenty of support from the rest of his team. Kyle Lowry bookended his scoreless Game 1 in this series by scoring the team's first nine points and had 12 points in the opening quarter. Lowry finished with 14 points and nine assists, drawing three charges on the defensive end and finished a plus-31 when he was on the court.

Toronto's stout defense was once again on display. The Magic missed 10 of their first 11 shots and missed all seven of their three-pointers in the period. The Raptors raced out to an 22-3 lead and led by 16 points after one quarter and never relented.

"Kyle played great tonight," Leonard said afterwards. "He got us all going with that amazing first quarter. We all just fed off his energy."

Toronto's first half was beautiful to watch. They recorded 19 assists on their 23 made field goals, which was a Raptors record for any single half in a postseason game. The Raptors finished with 34 assists, also a team playoff record.

"We kind of figured it out and made a good adjustment after Game 1," Lowry said afterwards. "We were a little bit too soft in coverages and we figured it out really quickly, what we wanted to do, how we needed to help each other and how we needed to play. To figure it out that quick is a really good thing for us. We've just got to continue to build off it."

Pascal Siakam was once again brilliant on both ends of the floor, finishing with 24 points on 8-of-16 shooting, making 3-of-5 from three, and adding six rebounds, four assists, and a block. Five Raptors players scored in double figures.

After a disappointing Game 1 performance, the Raptors got a glimpse at what Masai Ujiri had envisioned when he traded for Leonard and later acquired Marc Gasol at the trade deadline. Leonard as the leader, Lowry as the heartbeat, Siakam as the emerging star, and Gasol as the defensive anchor down low. Throughout the series,

Toronto Raptors small forward Norman Powell drives to the basket, defended by Orlando Magic big man Khem Birch.

Gasol frustrated All-Star centre Nikola Vucevic, who finished Game 5 with six points in 17 minutes, ending a frustrating playoff round against the former Defensive Player of the Year.

Nick Nurse was not surprised by his team's performance in Game 5, especially not Leonard's outstanding box score in a closeout match. "He's been through this before," Nurse told reporters afterwards. "The playoffs, and he's made deep runs, obviously. He relishes this time of the year and I think it shows. Playing strong, playing fast, playing defense. He's a great two-way player. He's a great player in this league."

The praise was not only directed towards Leonard. Nurse showed an appreciation for how his point guard bounced back from Game 1 and took control for the rest of the series. "He was amazing in this series," Nurse said of Lowry. "I don't know how many charges he ended up taking, but he was blocking out, taking charges, pushing the ball, getting in the paint, stroked just enough threes. He was maybe as good as I have never seen in this series."

Up next: a second round showdown with the Philadelphia 76ers. ■

EASTERN CONFERENCE SEMINALS, GAME 1

Raptors 108, 76ers 95
April 27, 2019 • Toronto, Ontario

OFF AND RUNNING

Raptors Look to Set the Tone for the Series with a Rare Easy Game 1 Win

By Sean Woodley

Some words just aren't part of the Toronto Raptors' playoff lexicon. "Easy" may be the foremost example. Series-opening victories had been rare enough for the franchise; convincing ones were just about unheard of. For at least one night to open the second round, though, it seemed like easy might creep into the team's vocabulary for a couple weeks.

Kawhi Leonard spent the spring squashing preconceived notions about the Raptors and the postseason. So maybe it's no surprise that he busted open the Sixers so casually in Toronto's 108-95 Game 1 win. He didn't waste time carving open a Sixers defense that would prove nearly impenetrable in the days to come. Apart from a bit of a sticky start for Toronto's offense and an early 7-2 Sixers run, the home side was the controlling owner of the game's flow. At the end of a 39-31 first quarter that saw the Raptors string together a run of 14-straight successful offensive possessions, Leonard had already posted 17 of his eventual 45 points on the night on a tasty 7-of-9 mark from the field.

He wasn't alone in his all-out Sixers evisceration. Matching Leonard point-for-point, shot-for-shot, was Pascal Siakam.

There's a case for Kawhi Leonard and Pascal Siakam having been unmatched as a duo around the league to that point in the playoffs. North of 50 points a game

against the Magic had come from the hands the Raptors' two top offensive options. With their success tearing into Philly in the opening 12 minutes of the series, it seemed as though maybe a formula of stout defense and a two-headed scoring monster would be enough against the paper-thin Sixers. Only five points were produced by guys not named Leonard or Siakam in the first frame and Toronto still led by eight. Surely their two-pronged dominance would last forever, right?

Helping matters was the obvious discomfort of Philadelphia's best player, Joel Embiid. Embiid missed the third game of his team's opening round win over the Brooklyn Nets to nurse a knee injury that held him out of a string of games late in the Sixers' season. He still wasn't right in Game 1. Adding to his personal pain was the guy lined up across from him in the paint, Marc Gasol. At the February 7th trade deadline, when the Raptors acquired Gasol in exchange for Jonas Valanciunas, Delon Wright, and a second-round pick, it was almost too obvious that it was done with Embiid in mind. Though Embiid's spent much of his career bullying whichever poor big man draws his assignment on a given night, Gasol had historically been the paper to Embiid's rock. In five previous regular season matchups, Gasol had limited Embiid to a piddly 14 points a game on a field-goal percentage that almost looked like a typo: 34.4. Gasol

Pascal Siakam and Kawhi Leonard were a powerhouse pair in Game 1, combining for 74 of the Raptors' 108 points.

wasn't some random trade target. And yet, even with Gasol walling off Embiid from easy buckets, the Sixers, as would become the tale of the series, were still great when Embiid was on the court, and an unending toilet swirl when he sat.

The second quarter saw coaches Nick Nurse and Brett Brown have their rotation patterns tested. Nurse came in as the traditionalist, starting second quarters with bench-heavy, less reliable lineups, as most teams tend to do. Brown, meanwhile, his hand forced by a slim-pickings set of reserves, was a little more kooky with his subs, often countering those more plush Raptors lineups with Embiid-led, starter-rich units. The result: each team would inevitably come across stretches during which a glaring advantage absolutely had to be pressed.

With Gasol having played the opening 9:27 of the first, only about half of which came against Embiid, Serge Ibaka found himself opposite Philly's post-up machine to open the second frame — a span that proved to be the hairiest the Raptors would encounter all night. Any hint of post-game fan angst towards Nurse was directly tied to this stretch. Embiid playing just 30 minutes meant it wouldn't have been that hard to have Gasol match him, minute-for-minute. But Nurse, unlike his predecessor Dwane Casey, is not about bending to the will of the opponent. He, at least for one game, was going to give Ibaka a chance to bang with Embiid.

"I think certainly for sure it's something he's earned," said Nurse of why he opted to trust Ibaka with the Embiid check into the second half despite a rocky second quarter that saw the Sixers claw to within one point.

"As the game wears on he always seems to get better and better," Nurse added, alluding to Ibaka's spritely second half in which he kept the dam from bursting. "We can't play Marc the whole game so we gotta get him out there. He was really something down the stretch,

blocking shots, and rebounding, and making some hard drives, and he definitely got in the rhythm of the game there in the fourth quarter."

Game 1 essentially ended when Embiid was forced to sit after a threatening start to the fourth quarter. Brown brought in the very green Jonah Bolden to play backup centre, and the Sixers got blitzed.

It was a sequence that highlighted what became the central struggle of the series will be for Philadelphia: Embiid had to sit at some point, and there was no security net to keep the bottom from caving in when he did so. Even with the job Gasol and Ibaka did disrupt his grace-plus-power post game (Embiid finished with 16 points on 5-of-18 shooting), the Sixers were plus-4 in his 30 minutes. Toronto won the game by 13.

The terms of the series appeared set over the course of the opening 48 minutes. Embiid would likely win his minutes; Toronto had to cruise when he sat; and Leonard and Siakam had to carry the offensive load in lieu while the supporting cast sorted through its persistent shooting troubles. Game 1 made it seem like a simple equation to replicate three more times for Toronto.

But remember, the Toronto Raptors don't do easy. ∎

Kawhi Leonard rejects Philadelphia 76ers forward Tobias Harris during the second half of the Game 1 win.

76ers 94, Raptors 89
April 29, 2019 • Toronto, Ontario

FALLING SHORT

Raptors Claw Back from Big Deficit but Can't Catch Philly in Game 2

By Sean Woodley

Ah, that's right. *This* is what playoff basketball is supposed to feel like.

If Game 1 of Raptors/Sixers was an outdoor acoustic show in a park, Game 2 was a metal show in a basement venue beneath a bowling alley. It was sweaty, compact, and mean. It's a wonder nobody lost an eye.

Brett Brown spent the day off between Games 1 and 2 ruminating on the loss, cooking up alterations to help give his team a better chance of winning the minutes with Joel Embiid on the floor; the minutes without him were always going to be a lost cause. The Sixers flashed two big changes out of the gates in Game 2. First, Joel Embiid was taken off of Marc Gasol and tasked with guarding Kawhi Leonard's right-hand man, Pascal Siakam, who with 29 Game 1 points had bumped his nightly postseason scoring average up to 23.7. And in place of Jimmy Butler, who bore the brunt of most of Leonard's Game 1 outburst, Philly's enormous, shot-afraid point guard Ben Simmons drew the toughest assignment one could possibly draw in the 2019 playoffs. If he couldn't stifle Leonard at least a little bit, the Sixers were surely toast.

One adjustment worked better than the other. After a promising first possession from Siakam, where he turned Embiid into the latest victim of his silky spin move, it looked as though he'd remain unfettered in spite of Embiid's comical largeness. Not so much. Over the remainder of the game, Siakam traded in his typical high-grade efficiency for bricks, finishing the night with 21 points on a lopsided 9-of-25 shooting line. Embiid had him spooked.

Leonard still did his thing, but Simmons nobly made him work for every single inch of space he needed to post 35 points, seven rebounds, and six assists. Considering Leonard's lofty standards, his barely-above .500 13-of-24 clip from the field stands an achievement in defense. Philly's oppressiveness extended to the rest of the Raptors as well. If you wipe away Leonard's contributions, Toronto shot a combined 20-of-66 on the night. Only one other Raptor — Kyle Lowry — joined Leonard and Siakam in scoring double digits; he finished with a vital 20-5-5.

Without Leonard's well-earned production, Toronto would have had no chance of lingering within striking distance into the late stages of the game. Matters were complicated by the arrival of some bench reinforcements on the Sixers' side. James Ennis offer up 13 points and six boards, while Greg Monroe — a Raptor up until the trade deadline — looked for a moment like the solution to Philly's lack of backup big men with 10 points in 11 minutes.

But there the Raptors were, having chipped away at what was a 19-point Sixers lead with 4:18 to play in the second quarter, stuck just six points behind heading into the fourth.

A small detail about the Sixers that you'd have been forgiven for forgetting before the final 12 minutes of Game 2: Philadelphia traded for Jimmy Butler earlier in the season. Butler, a notorious Raptor killer throughout his career (he once broke a Michael Jordan record with 40 points in a single half in a game against Toronto in 2016), was brought in to be Philly's closer, and boy did he ever live up to his job description in Game 2. Butler canned 12 of his 30 points over the course of the final

Kyle Lowry draws a foul on Philadelphia 76ers forward Tobias Harris while driving to the basket during the second half.

frame, going a perfect 5-of-5 from the line as well. Every Raptors punch met a mean Butler counter.

"This was James Butler," said Brown after the game. "That was the adult in the gym ... He was just a tremendous sort of rock."

"My name isn't James. It's literally Jimmy." Butler responded, deadpan.

Toronto's last attempt to break through and even the game came in the form of a Lowry triple, a Tobias Harris turnover on the other end, and a Siakam rebound and put-back of his own miss that cut the lead to 90-89 with 46 seconds to play. Butler needed someone to match his will to snatch the potentially series-saving win.

Prior to Game 2, it wasn't entirely clear whether the fulcrum of the entire series, Embiid, would even play. A bout of gastroenteritis rendered him questionable in the lead up to opening tip. He played, though not especially well until it was absolutely necessary. With a drive and a stutter-step into a finish through Siakam and Gasol —

probably the biggest play of his career — Embiid put the Sixers up by three with just 24 seconds to play.

Embiid bluntly joked about the symptoms of his illness when asked how he was feeling after Game 2. "But these are my guys and I want to show up every night and play hard."

Still, Toronto, through a night of deficient offense and Embiid and Butler's late heroics, had a chance to tie the game and force overtime. You couldn't ask for a better look than the one they got, either. Kyle Lowry, ever cheeky, tried and failed to slip a dribble through the legs of Harris, inciting a mad scramble for the loose ball. Through the chaos, Danny Green, the NBA's second-most accurate long-range shooter in the regular season, had acres of space to pull up and release the shot.

Iron. Sixers rebound. Game. Philly had taken home court advantage away, the series set to head back to the hostile Wells Fargo Center. This was going to be a series. ■

76ers 116, Raptors 95
May 2, 2019 • Philadelphia, Pennsylvania

LOSING CONTROL

Raptors Take One on the Chin in Game 3, Lose by 21 to Philly

By Sean Woodley

Toronto had yet to be truly kicked in the teeth through seven games of playoff action. Sure, the D.J. Augustin game-winner to kick off the Magic series was annoying for fans, but the Raptors as a team seemed to be entirely unperturbed. Their subsequent schooling of Orlando over the next four games proved as much.

Losing a coin flip game to the Sixers at home also stung. Adorning the edges of the box score in silver, however, was the knowledge that despite Toronto doing just about everything it could do to lose Game 1, it was a missed three from a three-point specialist away from overtime. Joel Embiid's knee was presumably still sore; Ben Simmons was still defiant in his opposition to shooting anything but layups; Greg Monroe couldn't possibly be considered a viable answer to Philly's issues backing up Embiid. Even without home court advantage, you could argue the Raptors still had control of the series.

Any notions of comfort or confidence would be obliterated by the end of Game 3 in Philadelphia.

Jimmy Butler was spectacular, once again, nearly posting a triple-double with 22 points, nine rebounds, and nine assists on a tight 9-of-15 shooting. Philly's home crowd was raucous enough to spark debate back in Toronto about why the famously loud Raptors crowd was losing its thunder.

Most troubling for Toronto though, is that Embiid appeared to have overcome both his wretched bowels and his achy knee in just two days. If any lingering discomfort still dogged his huge frame, the energy of the building ushered him through it. Embiid was in the kind of zone

that supersedes smart coaching or great defensive effort. Game 3 marked the beginning of Nurse's slow inching towards matching Gasol up against Embiid minute-for-minute. Philly's fringe-MVP candidate responded to that by scoring a series-best 33 points on 18 shots; he grabbed 10 boards, dished three assists, and swatted five hopeless Toronto shots away as well. The implications of the latter stat impressed his coach the most.

"For me it goes straight to the blocks," Brett Brown said in assessment of Embiid's masterclass. "We could talk about a windmill dunk, you could talk about some finesse post moves and that. But I go to defense … He is our crown jewel defensively, and I suppose offensively too but certainly defensively, and his rim protection and blocking shot ability tonight stood out as much as anything in an incredible performance."

Philadelphia's lead see-sawed between cozy and precarious through three quarters, but it was never surrendered. The sternest challenge to the Sixers' vice-grip over Game 3 came in the closing moments of the third as Kawhi Leonard started Kawhi Leonard-ing. At the 8:16 mark of the third, the Sixers held a commanding 18-point edge. At that instant, Leonard posted the first of his 14 points in the quarter. It took just six attempts, all makes, for Leonard to compile them. Toronto trailed 89-81 after three.

A spell on the bench for Leonard loomed to open the final quarter. He'd already accrued 32 high-leverage minutes to that point and was a made free throw show of a point-per-minute pace. Nurse sat him, Fred VanVleet drained a technical foul shot carried over from the

Joel Embiid goes flying as he attempts to wrest control of the ball from Kawhi Leonard. The Raptors had no answer for Embiid's Game 3 masterclass.

previous quarter, and Toronto had to weather a Leonard-less storm, ideally without seeing their seven-point deficit balloon past being manageable.

The mouth-kick the Raptors had avoided all spring was nigh. A measly 2 minutes and 23 seconds of rest for Leonard came at the cost of a game-sealing 9-0 run, during which time a frustrated Pascal Siakam bone headedly tripped Embiid with an outstretched leg. While the flagrant foul call hurt, the real damage was done to Siakam's calf, though that wouldn't be revealed for another two days. Upon Leonard's return to the floor, Embiid crammed down a windmill dunk with a brazenness the Raptors hadn't been exposed to since LeBron James spun a ball in Serge Ibaka's face before draining a three a year prior. Apart from Leonard's individual brilliance, Game 3, more than any other over

the course of Toronto's championship run, felt like a chapter from the book of the Same Old Raptors.

"We've got to help him. We've got to help him," Kyle Lowry said of his superhuman teammate after the 21-point loss. "Myself especially, I've got to help him score more. I've got to help him on the floor. We've all got to help him. He's playing unbelievable right now. We're not giving him any help. Me, I'm not giving him any help. We've got to help him."

By end of Game 3, Joel Embiid's bout of indigestion had been transferred to the guts of the entire Raptors fan base. While a familiar feeling, it was certainly not a welcome one. Game 4 would, more-or-less, be about saving the season. ∎

Raptors 101, 76ers 96
May 5, 2019 • Philadelphia, Pennsylvania

REASON TO BELIEVE

Raptors Respond in Game 4, Even Things Up Heading Back to Toronto

By Sean Woodley

What's a playoff run without wild, irrational swings of emotion?

Just eight days after Toronto's euphoric, resistance-free win in the opener, the team found itself staring down the barrel of a 3-1 disadvantage, its massive off-season gambles hanging very much in the balance. Game 4 against Philly was wrought with all the accompanying impending sense of doom Raptors fans know better than most anyone else. And some troublesome news in the lead up to tip-off didn't help matters calm the nerves.

Just over 24 hours before game time, word came down that Pascal Siakam was dealing with a calf contusion, and was listed doubtful for the first of many Biggest Games in Franchise History the Raptors would contest during their run. People's minds immediately rushed back to his dirty trip of Embiid in the previous game — did that play, with the game out of reach, really just cost Toronto it's best chance of making it to the NBA Finals? With the Raptors' bench having been M.I.A. for three games, the likelihood of Toronto having the juice to survive a Siakam absence seemed slim.

Credit to Siakam. In the lead-up to game time, he was ruled to be active. He started, and while clearly hobbled, gutted out 29 minutes. It almost doesn't matter that he scored just 9 points on 2-of-10 from the floor; he provided something the Raptors desperately needed that day: a warm body.

"I don't want to say it limited me. I have no excuse if I'm out there on the floor," Siakam said afterwards. "That means I am ready to play. Maybe a little lateral movement a little bit just because it was sore and also my hamstring was sore. Those two combined it's kind of like it makes it a little tough for you to move or be as active as you want to be."

No matter how much Siakam insists his calf didn't hinder him, it was clear as day that he was not his usual explosive self. Filling in the gaps left behind by a sub-standard Siakam was Serge Ibaka — the first Toronto reserve to do much of anything in the series. His 12 points, nine rebounds, and three blocks were essential. His awakening from a series-long slumber opened up a scale-tipping avenue for Nick Nurse to travel down.

Contrary to the popular small-skewing ways of NBA in 2019, Game 4 saw Nurse opt for enormity. Serge Ibaka and Marc Gasol had scantily played together since the two Spanish national teammates were united in Toronto. The playoffs force coaches to defy their own instincts. Philadelphia's entire ethos is centred on being huge; to save the season, Nurse had to deviate from the centre platoon he'd rolled out all year and fight size with size.

Ibaka and Gasol played nearly half the game side-

Kyle Lowry argues for a call during what was a hard-fought Game 4 Raptors win.

by-side, with a lot of those minutes coming in one of the most intense stretches of crunch time in Raptors history. In seven fourth quarter minutes, a Lowry / Green / Leonard / Ibaka / Gasol fivesome held the Sixers to fewer than half a point scored per possession. Philly didn't hold back their best guys. Both Butler and Harris played all 12 minutes in the quarter; Embiid and Simmons played 10 apiece. It was a quarter ripped straight out of a monster movie, giants wailing on each other, back and forth. Not once in the first 11:30 of the quarter was either team ahead by more than two possessions. The game was thirsty for a moment.

Kawhi Leonard has a knack for moments.

Toronto's offense ran into some mud in the fourth quarter. The Leonard-Gasol pick-and-roll was about the only trick the team had left in the bag. Possession-after-possession, Gasol would hit Leonard's man, Simmons, with a screen; Joel Embiid would switch onto Leonard in space, and Leonard did what we could to scrape out buckets against one of the most imposing defenders in basketball. With 1:06 remaining and the score 91-90 for Toronto, the script repeated itself again. Gasol tagged Simmons and Embiid picked up Leonard. This time, instead of driving into traffic the way he'd routinely done earlier on, Leonard stepped back, one second on the shot clock, and launched a three over the outstretched arm of Embiid. Cash.

"I came off the pick-and-roll and they tried to stagger us. Jo is a good defender, really long," explained Leonard post-game. "At the time I looked up at the shot clock and tried to create as much space as possible. I just took a shot and believed it would go in, and it did."

It did, and the Raptors hung on for 60 seconds to take Game 4 and reclaim home court. Leonard believed it would go in. Raptors fans had reason to believe, period. ∎

Kawhi Leonard splits through multiple 76ers defenders on his way to the hoop. Leonard rose to the occasion with buckets in key moments to even up the series.

Raptors 125, 76ers 89
May 7, 2019 · Toronto, Ontario

PHILLY NOT SO SPECIAL

Toronto Destroys Philadelphia in Game 5 Laugher

By Sean Woodley

Toronto was favored to beat Philadelphia going into their second round series for a reason. The Raptors were deeper, better on both offense and defense in the regular season, and had the consensus best player in Kawhi Leonard. Philadelphia probably outgunned Toronto when it came to top-end talent — Jimmy Butler, and Joel Embiid are All-Stars; Ben Simmons will be one day; even Tobias Harris put together a decent case to earn a spot in a loaded Western Conference before he was dealt to Philly. But it was that trade (and the Butler deal before that) that left the Sixers with a far more unstable chemical makeup than Toronto. The latter had congealed into a swarming and scoring monster with the addition of the binding agent that was Marc Gasol. Philly hadn't even really established an obvious hierarchy for touches.

All those advantages and more were pressed by the Raptors in Game 5.

Toronto didn't need another Leonard explosion to take a boot to Philly that Tuesday night at Scotiabank Arena. After a closely contested 27-26 first quarter, the Raptors cruised on the back of six guys in double figures and, finally, more than one bench player chipping in a passable performance.

Philly lost touch over the course of a 37-17 second quarter by Toronto on the strength of Nurse's new toy:

the jumbo front court. Ibaka and Gasol combined for the first four buckets of the quarter, Toronto's half-court defense crested, holding the Sixers to just 6 makes on 20 shots in the frame, and Leonard capped the quarter with the first of two thunderous dunks he'd jam that night. Both Harris and James Ennis are immortal now, in poster form. Embiid had his soul snatched a quarter later.

Game 5 proved to be the worst effort Embiid would pump out over the course of the series, as his knee concerns bubbled up to the surface once again. His eight turnovers were three more than the number of times he filled the bucket, and his -15 proved to be the only negative plus-minus total he accrued in the entire series. Even with a fully functioning Embiid, the Sixers toed a precarious line whenever he'd sit. A bad Embiid game left the Sixers without a prayer.

"Oh yeah. He was playing. He was trying to play hard, help his team get W," said Ibaka when asked if Embiid appeared to be at full health. "I think we just do a great job as a team to make everything tough for him. Every time he's catching the ball in the post we made sure he had to work for every basket."

Things were so stacked against the Sixers that even Danny Green had himself a night. The 2019 playoffs were a stark deviation from Green's regular season. For stretches between October and April, it seemed as though

Kawhi Leonard dunks over Joel Embiid, taking advantage of what was an off night for the 76ers star.

Green couldn't possibly miss. Toronto finished tops in the league in scoring efficiency in transition largely on the back of Green being money on the break. His drop from 45.5 percent to 35.5 percent from the season to the first nine games of the postseason was troubling enough. What happened to him in the games following his 5-of-7 outing from long range in Game 5 is a mystery that may never be solved. But for one night, he was party to a Raptors' onslaught. In fact, the 36-point thumping would stand — for a short time — as the most bloated victory in franchise history. A Game 6 in Philly lurked on the horizon, but Game 5 truly felt at the time like the Raptors had realized they were a better team, and acted on it. Good thing momentum always carries over from game to game in the NBA playoffs. ■

Above: Marc Gasol and Kawhi Leonard share a laugh on the bench during the second half. Opposite: Joel Embiid unsuccessfully tries to prevent a Pascal Siakam dunk. Siakam scored a team-high 25 points in Game 5.

EASTERN CONFERENCE SEMINALS, GAME 6

76ers 112, Raptors 101
May 9, 2019 • Philadelphia, Pennsylvania

THE PRESSURE'S ON

76ers Respond to Game 5 Drubbing, Square Series at 3-3

By Sean Woodley

Typically when two teams are closely matched, the games within a long series between them will play out as such. Toronto and Philadelphia marched to a different beat. Rather than engaging in drawn-out, high-intensity duels defined by jabs and clinches and ending in narrow decisions, the Raptors and 76ers took turns trading game-deciding haymakers in the opening minutes of their bouts.

Toronto's latest knockout blow in Game 5 really shouldn't have been one from which the Sixers could recover. A 36-point waxing to force a do-or-die elimination game might have broken the spirit of lesser teams; it certainly would have spelled the end for past iterations of the Toronto Raptors. These Sixers were a resilient bunch, though. And they had home court for Game 6.

Early on in the penultimate game of the series, it looked as though the Raptors might be buried by a quick Sixers barrage. Three consecutive Jimmy Butler buckets landed the Raptors in a 13-5 hole when Nick Nurse called his first timeout to settle things down. Wells Fargo Center went ballistic.

Out of the break, Toronto bucked the series-long trend of teams laying down at the first sign of trouble. Forcing either a miss or turnover on nine straight Sixers possessions, the Raptors quickly rattled off a 10-0 run to inch them ahead by two.

They would not lead the game again.

Philly punched back with might, and each subsequent Raptors' attempt to close the gap would be parried away with relative ease.

"It was kind of a strange game of runs, where they came out and blasted us and we crawled back in, and then they went right back again on maybe an 8-0 run or something like that," Nurse described. "There was just too many fast momentum swings."

Any stretches wherein Toronto flirted with an earnest comeback in Game 6 coincided with Boban Marjanovic's barely coordinated 7'3 frame filling in for Joel Embiid. Brett Brown simply responded to those spurts of Boban-induced trouble by subbing Embiid back in. Toronto wilted in response, every time.

Embiid's pedestrian 17-points, 12-rebound effort on 5-of-14 shooting does not capture the all-encompassing grip the big man held over the game, and really the series as a whole. In a game Philly won by 11, the Sixers were plus-40 in Embiid's 36 minutes of floor time. Marjanovic was minus-18 in six minutes. Embiid's wobbly knee was a long way from the palm of his hand, the place in which the entirety of the series could be found. If only he could just play a full-48.

Toronto's three best players were once again marooned on their lonesome island of productivity. Leonard, Lowry, and Siakam's efforts comprised 63 of the Raptors' 101 points, while the already listing supporting cast plummeted nose-first into the sea. The utility of the Ibaka-Gasol pairing faded. If they weren't going to play to their size and manage more than a single offensive rebound in 13 minutes together, what was the point, really? They got bludgeoned on the defensive glass, too. The only thing steady about Fred VanVleet was becoming his knack for getting shut out

The Raptors missed a big opportunity to close out the series in Game 6, falling 112-101 to the 76ers and forcing a deciding Game 7 in Toronto.

from the floor; he was 0-of-1 in 16 minutes.

Meanwhile, Philadelphia's ill-fitting stars coalesced into something that spelled doom for future iterations of the Eastern Conference. Ben Simmons, mostly relegated to Leonard duty on defense and Butler-watching on the other end through five games, snatched control of the game's pace from the jump.

"I think our poor shooting got him out in the open floor a lot," Nurse said in assessment of Simmons's 21-point, eight-rebound, six-assist performance. "I thought he made a lot more straight line, non-hesitant moves tonight. When he started to go, he started to go."

With Simmons' late arrival to the series, the top-end talent disparity between the two squads revealed itself in full, robust light. When Philly's stars played like that, the Raptors — or any team, really — were in trouble.

A Game 7 now stood, menacing in the painfully distant future. Two full days between Games 6 and 7 to ruminate on all the implications and history at play seemed downright abusive to a Raptors fan base that had endured so much torment in the past. The Raptors would be at home, and they'd be favoured. Something like 80-percent of Game 7s throughout history went to the team with the crowd in their corner.

But winner-take-all games throw data and the comfort of large sample sizes in the trash. By getting pummeled in Game 6, Toronto exposed itself to being done in by the cruelty of basketball's deities. Leonard's future, and by extension the course of the franchise for years to come would hinge on the result of a single 48-minute game back in Toronto.

No pressure. ■

EASTERN CONFERENCE SEMINALS, GAME 7

Raptors 92, 76ers 90
May 12, 2019 • Toronto, Ontario

FOURTH BOUNCE'S A CHARM

Leonard's Unlikely, Incredible Buzzer-Beater Sends Raps to Conference Finals

By Sean Woodley

Back in 2001, Vince Carter's Raptors took Allen Iverson's Sixers to a deciding seventh game in their second round playoff series. The morning of Game 7 in Philadelphia, Carter travelled with his mother on the private jet of Raptors controlling owner Larry Tanenbaum to Chapel Hill, North Carolina for his college graduation. He returned to Philadelphia afterwards to take on the Sixers with a spot in the Eastern Conference Finals against the Milwaukee Bucks on the line.

While the effect his travel that day has always been overstated by Carter's grumpiest critics, his day trip stuck in the craw of fans as the beginning of his prolonged separation from the city he helped put on the basketball map. At the end of a defensive battle of a Game 7 that saw Iverson and Carter both shoot poorly, Carter had an opportunity to ensure no one would ever callback to his graduation decision ever again. With 2.0 seconds on the clock and the Raptors down 88-87, Dell Curry inbounded the ball to Carter on the left wing. Without taking a dribble he stopped, shook off a beckoning Tyrone Hill with a pump fake, and launched an off-balance 21-footer. It was heavy. It pinged off the back half of the rim and bounced harmlessly away as time expired. Philadelphia advanced. Vince would never again play a postseason game in a Raptors jersey. (Toronto made the playoffs in 2002 after a thrilling stretch drive — Carter missed all of it with injury. He was traded to the Nets a season and a half later).

The ghosts of 2001 lingered in the rafters of Toronto's Scotiabank Arena ahead of Game 7 of the same round against the same team 18 years later. The circumstances were different.

Toronto was at home this time, and the Raptors' roster was far more stout than the collection of sage veterans that orbited around Carter back in '01. But the prize of a victory was the same: An Eastern Conference Finals date with the Milwaukee Bucks, and a realistic path to the NBA's championship series.

Toronto fans are fabled for their anxiety. At times during the DeMar DeRozan/Dwane Casey era, you could plainly observe the Raptors' players taking on the uneasiness of its fans in tight contests. ESPN NBA reporter Zach Lowe made talk of Toronto's collectively "tight sphincters" in the playoffs a running, entirely accurate joke for years. No previous Raptor game — not the Game 7 against Brooklyn in 2014, not either of the two winner-take-all games contested on the road to the 2016 conference finals, not even the doomed Game 1 against Cleveland one year prior — was smothered in a layer of tension as thick as the one blanketing version 2.0 of Game 7 against the Sixers.

Kawhi Leonard's improbable game-winner was the most memorable in Raptors history and one of the best shots in the history of NBA playoff basketball.

Mercifully for neutrals, the game unfolded in a similar fashion to Games 2 and 4: rugged, defensive, never out of reach one way or another, stressful as can be.

The first quarter reeked of fear. Or maybe it was just great defense. Toronto entered the quarter break with an 18-13 lead, a 12-minute score pulled straight from a Pistons-Pacers classic out of the mid-aughts. Toronto looked and felt like the better team at first, holding the Sixers off the scoreboard for four-and-a-half minutes to open the game. Alas, when a J.J. Redick three notched the first Sixers points, the score was only 6-3 in Toronto's favour. The home side was ice cold. Earlier in the day, Portland and Denver's usually excellent offenses contested a similarly grimy Game 7 out West. There's a script these types of games have always followed, and the Raptors and Sixers left no room for improv.

No team led by more than nine points at any point. Heading into the deciding fourth quarter, Philly had chipped away a point-per-quarter off the Raptors' 5-point lead through one. Putrid as it was, the 36.5 field goal percentage posted by the Sixers was the better shooting mark of the two sides. Kawhi Leonard emptied his clip, and had a 10-of-30 mark to show for it with 12 minutes left to play. If the game were a food, it would have been prison gruel.

A constant throughout was Nick Nurse, after flirting with it over the last few games, going full bore in matching Marc Gasol's minutes with Joel Embiids. Brown couldn't trust anyone but his superstar big man to anchor the team. Nurse couldn't trust anyone but Gasol to make his life difficult. The result was a pair of exhausted seven-footers.

"Yeah, I think the minutes things for both teams are going to be off the table," Nurse mentioned the day before Game 7. "So, I would expect the best players to play absolutely as many minutes as they possibly can all the way through until it's decided."

Embiid played a series-high 45:12 of 48 minutes. Gasol lined up across from him for every single one of

Joel Embiid stands in disbelief while Leonard, his teammates, and Raptors fans are euphoric after the amazing series-clinching shot.

those 2,532 seconds. Philly won the Embiid minutes by 10 points. It was the other 2:48 that were the problem.

For all the preparation and strategery that goes on in the lead up, Game 7s are often decided by fluky nonsense. Both Toronto and Philadelphia can attest. Coming into the night, Serge Ibaka had gone without a made three-pointer since Game 4 of the Orlando series — 10 consecutive missed attempts, many of them miles from going in. Naturally, he accounted for three of Toronto's seven made triples on the night … on five attempts. The last of them he drilled in the face of Ben Simmons, striking a dramatic pose upon the landing. Style points are important. He finished the night with 17 points, eight rebounds, three assists, and was a team-best plus-22. Only Ibaka posted a shooting percentage above 50 for the Raptors.

"Oh, he was huge man," said Danny Green of Ibaka's efforts in Game 7. "He was on the glass, offensive rebounds, defensive rebounds, blocking shots, making things difficult, and hitting threes. Kind of looked like me out there in the corner one time. A little pump fake, swing through and no dribble shot. I've never seen him do that one before, but it was good to see."

Ibaka's swaggerful triple came with 9:37 left to play in fourth quarter. It stood as the game's most iconic shot for exactly nine minutes and thirty-seven seconds.

With 4.2 seconds remaining and the score tied at 90, Kawhi Leonard had the opportunity to do what Vince Carter could not: finish off the Sixers with a single made bucket.

Toronto probably shouldn't have even been in the situation it found itself. Eight seconds of game time earlier, Leonard had a chance to put the Raptors up three my making the second of two free throws. He clanged it, and tried to crash to glass the collect his miss. Jimmy Butler pounced on Leonard's ill-timed aggressiveness, retrieved the ball, and streaked coast-to-coast for a layup that tied the game, threatening to send the game to an overtime that not one person in the 19,800-strong crowd would have felt good about. The bucket was the first Philly had mustered in minutes, as Toronto's swarming,

recovering, and suffocating defense stymied smothered Philly in the half court all throughout crunch time, forcing a pair of shot clock violations and nearly a third.

"Tenacious, tough, switching," Brown said of Toronto's late-game D. "One through five was a switch group and we had a hard time turning the corner. I thought we passed up a few shots that we could've shot and the clock evaporated. I thought that maybe we got a little too greedy, but give Toronto credit."

After a Raptors timeout, the ball was advanced to the left hashmark at the west end of the floor. Marc Gasol's sure hands got the ball in to Leonard, who dribbled right. Simmons was soon joined by Embiid in the effort to keep Leonard away from open space — and the pair succeeded. With just four tenths of a second on the clock, Leonard, contained in the right corner, pulled up and arched a high rainbow over the outstretched hand of the 7'2 Embiid. Leonard crouched in the corner to watch the flight of the ball. An arena sat silent, waiting to erupt. The ball bounced once, high, straight up. The comedown took a lifetime. It bounced again, with a lower amplitude and to the left. A third bounce, this time on the other side of the rim, any further towards the back lip and it probably goes the way of Vince's miss in 2001. And then a fourth bounce. This time, the ball was resigned to its ultimate destination: the bottom of the bucket.

Bedlam.

The shot went in. Somehow. The Raptors had won the series. Somehow. With the win, the Leonard experiment was vindicated in full. Sports fans spend a lifetime waiting for a moment as unexpected and euphoric as the one Toronto's mercenary superstar provided with his pinball bucket — the first ever series-clinching buzzer-beater in a Game 7. The Raptors were moving on to the Eastern Conference Finals to play Milwaukee. Leonard's immortality in Toronto was sealed. ∎

Leonard's shot was the first series-clinching buzzer-beater in a Game 7 in NBA history. In that moment, Leonard cemented his place in Canadian sports lore.

Bucks 108, Raptors 100
May 15, 2019 · Milwaukee, Wisconsin

BACK TO SQUARE ONE

Raptors Find Themselves in a Familiar 1-0 Hole After Loss in Milwaukee

By Sean Woodley

Toronto found itself in an unfamiliar spot heading into the Eastern Conference Finals against the Milwaukee Bucks.

For the first time in the postseason, Toronto wasn't burdened by the expectations that come with being favored. With just two off days between series, the city-wide high Kawhi Leonard induced with his miracle buzzer-beater had barely even worn off in Toronto. Milwaukee's 60 regular season wins led the league, they boasted the likely league MVP in Giannis Antetokounmpo, and their advanced statistics painted the picture of a historically dominant title favorite. Home court tends to come in handy in the postseason as well; advantage Bucks in that department, too. Barring an embarrassing exit in four or five games, there would have been no shame in the Raptors falling to the league's supreme darlings of 2019.

Toronto's start in Game 1 indicated early that the teams were far more closely matched than original prognostications suggested. A commitment to sprinting out off of Bucks misses and a healthy diet of long-range shots saw the Raptors race out to a 34-23 lead on the Bucks' home floor. Kawhi Leonard and Pascal Siakam chipped in nine points each. No big deal.

What was really encouraging on the Toronto side of the ledger was the aggression of Kyle Lowry and Marc Gasol. Both hampered by passiveness when the Sixers would gift wrap them open looks at the basket, the pair fired away whenever open against their new, less physically imposing opponent. Against Milwaukee, a team that attempted more threes than every team but one in the regular season, Toronto made a concerted effort to tilt the math equation in its favour from beyond the arc. More than half of the Raptors' looks in the opening 12 minutes were threes; they went 6-of-13.

Milwaukee spent the middle quarters pecking away at the cushion Toronto built up early. They didn't do so through their typical brand of high-octane offense, though. Antetokounmpo and Middleton, the Bucks' two most steady sources of reliable offense, were stifled by Toronto's defensive plan of attack. Toronto swarmed Antetokounmpo with fury any time he made a foray to the rim, often meeting him with three of four bodies. Five turnovers marred the Buck's superstar's otherwise solid 24-14-6 line for the game. Middleton finished the game with just 11 points on 4-of-11 shooting, as he drew the undesirable task of scoring with Leonard stapled to him as a primary defender.

Middleton's work as Leonard's guard at the other end, however, more than made up for his off-shooting evening. Even when Leonard found success, it was hard-earned. His 14-point third quarter, for example, required 12 shots and four trips to the line to accrue.

"We talk about defense, defense, defense," said Bucks coach Mike Budenholzer. "There are going to be nights when you don't make shots, and you've got to just continue to do well or give it defensively. If you do that, you maybe can break through and find a way to win on a night when you really don't shoot very well."

Only one Raptor was truly able to bust out of the Bucks' clamps. Kyle Lowry, notorious for his no-shows in Game 1s — even as recently as his pointless playoff-opener against Orlando a month prior — turned in one of the most complete efforts of his postseason career. Nursing a sprained left thumb that forced him to wear an oven mitt-like circulation glove nearly any time he wasn't actually playing, Lowry exploded for 30 points on 10-of-15 shooting and blistering 7-of-9 mark from downtown. Making his gaudy numbers more impressive was the fact that they mostly came against All-Defense First Team guard Eric Bledsoe.

"Yeah, he was really good," Nurse said of his point guard. "It's not easy. We talked about pregame, they've got a bunch of athletic guards and they run a bunch of guys at him and they're doing a decent job of limiting his touches. So I thought it was good that he could get the ball as much as he did."

Lowry's steady stream of buckets was accompanied by all the other unchartable accoutrements his game includes. One diving save of an errant Danny Green pass stood out in particular.

"He was fighting like heck out there," Nurse went on. "I thought he threw his body in front of people on a few things, didn't get the whistle on a few. He always draws charges and there were tons of charges going on out there, but he still was taking them. That's his thing. And he was good. He was awesome."

Nobody else on the Raptors warranted such praise after Game 1. As the game progressed, the Bucks' week of rest ahead of the series became an obvious factor in the proceedings. Toronto entered the fourth quarter with an 83-76 lead, and a chance to steal away home court in the series. They did not seize it.

Toronto's non-Lowry guys went quite literally as cold as humanly possible. Just five Raptors shots found the bottom of the basket in the final 12 minutes. Every single one came off the hands of Lowry. He missed just twice;

his teammates went 0-of-15. A single Pascal Siakam free throw along with a pair of Leonard makes from the stripe that put Toronto up 100-98 were all the help Lowry received on the offensive end.

Lowry's solo efforts weren't enough to ward off the inevitable Bucks surge. Brook Lopez caught fire for Milwaukee late. The NBA's single-season record holder for threes made by a seven-footer had just one to show for the opening three frames. He dropped three in the fourth on five tries, and posted 13 of his 29 points in the quarter. A 10-0 run for Milwaukee in the final three and a half minutes sealed the victory and the 1-0 series lead. You couldn't help but be reminded of a different missed opportunity for the Raptors in a critical Game 1 a year earlier.

At the end of a tightly-contested opener against the Cleveland Cavaliers in the 2018 Eastern Conference Semifinals, Fred VanVleet missed a wide-open three with the game tied and only a few seconds on the clock. His miss was followed by four straight bricked put backs by DeMar DeRozan and Jonas Valanciunas. The game went to overtime, and the Raptors fell 113-112 to lose an eminently winnable game against a team they were quantitatively far better than. The loss broke the Raptors. Dwane Casey referenced the unfortunate finish to the game after each and every one of the Raptors' subsequent three losses to be swept out of the playoffs by LeBron James... again. They could not get past it. Losing another game that was on a platter a year later may have been an insurmountable obstacle for the old Raptors.

But these were the new Raptors.

"It sucks when you lose like that. But we had a chance, and we've got to learn from it and make an adjustment," said a calm Lowry after the loss. "Stay even-keeled, never too high, never too low. Just look at the film and get better."

Toronto's resolve to power through hard times would again be tested in 48 hours' time. ∎

Bucks 125, Raptors 103
May 17, 2019 • Milwaukee, Wisconsin

TROUBLE BREWING

Raptors No-Show in Game 2, Face a Critical Game 3 at Home

By Sean Woodley

Some nights you just don't have it.

The Raptors surely hoped they wouldn't be afflicted by a bout of utter hopelessness on a night when a 2-0 series disadvantage hung intimidatingly over the game, but you can't always pick and choose when the gears are going to get stuck.

Frankly, Game 2 of the Eastern Conference Finals could have been called three minutes after tip, as the Bucks galloped to 9-0 lead that they'd only continue to build upon throughout the evening.

"You got your coverages and your things you're going to do at the beginning, and we just missed them early," said Nick Nurse of the lackluster start by Toronto. "We were just a step too slow on just about everything. I talked before the game about how important shot-contesting was. I just didn't think we settled in with some space, and we gave them confidence early. You just can't do that."

In diagnosing why the Raptors fell so flat in Game 2, the first area of focus would be Marc Gasol. In Game 1, Gasol was excellent for three quarters, quarterbacking the defense, going toe-to-toe with the NBA's dunk king, Antetokounmpo, and taking at least some of the uncontested shots available to him. As he cratered in the fourth quarter — on offense, on the glass, and around the rim — Toronto's odds of winning plummeted. He was even more dreadful the next time out.

Gasol made a career out of being one of the deftest passing big men in basketball history. His ability to bind together disparate parts of an offensive attack with his dishes and dimes was one of the reasons the Raptors found themselves in the Conference Finals, period. It

served as a bad omen, then, when midway through the first quarter, Gasol attempted to hit Kawhi Leonard on a basic high-low feed. Instead of finding a soft landing in the hands of Leonard under the hoop, the ball ricocheted off the bottom of the backboard into the hands of Antetokounmpo, who streaked the other way for his third thunderous dunk of the quarter. The play was symptomatic of the Raptors' team-wide disarray.

"I don't know, I feel bad for him," said a perplexed Nurse. "Most of those went in and out. It's like, he's a really good player, a really good scorer. He was taking good shots and just couldn't buy one."

Gasol's 1-of-9 shooting effort was secondary to the measly 19:21 of court time he saw in what was to that point his worst game in a Raptor uniform. His scaled back second half workload was partly a byproduct of the game being out of reach, but it could have also represented the early stages of a diminished trust on Nurse's part in Gasol's ability to hang in the Bucks matchup. Calls for a starting lineup change dominated the day off between Games 2 and 3, with the struggling Gasol at the centre of the outrage.

Of course, a 22-point shellacking is never the fault of just one man. Game 2 was on par with Games 3 and 6 against Philadelphia when it came to the number of duds laid up and down the roster. Lowry had one of his worst games of the postseason — a mostly ineffectual 15 points on 4-of-13 shooting and a decidedly un-Lowry-like minus-19 when on the court. Pascal Siakam, cruelly tasked with guarding and being guarded by Antetokounmpo after having to contend with Joel Embiid a series prior, fouled out before ever establishing an imprint on the game. His

Serge Ibaka wrestles for the ball with the Bucks' Giannis Antetokounmpo in the Game 2 loss. The Raptors were blown out in the game but wouldn't lose again in the Eastern Conference Finals.

issues staying in front of the Greek Freak inspired what ended up being Antetokounmpo's best game of the series: 30 points, 17 rebounds, and five assists with a couple blocks added in for fun.

Ironically enough, it was that performance that would spawn a series-altering adjustment from Nurse a game later.

Nurse had no answers in the moment of Game 2, though. A resilient third quarter push flirted with becoming a little interesting. Leonard was a casual supernova, navigating the rugged Bucks' defense en route to an efficient 15 points in the frame. Norman Powell, silent since the end of the first round, flashed a bit of spunk in the third as well. Powell awakening was cause for a least a touch of optimism heading into a virtual must-win Game 3. His history of tormenting the Bucks dated back to the opening round of the 2017 playoffs,

when his move into the starting five in a high-stakes Game 4 all but solved the series for Toronto.

"Yeah, it was good to see Norm," Nurse mentioned post-game. "I had planned on using him a lot more in the rotation. I think he fits in this series a little more (than vs. Philadelphia) with his speed and strength and athleticism, his ability to take it off the bounce. We're going to need that. It was good to get him going, and I would imagine going forward he'll be a critical part of the series for our rotation."

If Powell was going to return to utility in the Conference Finals, maybe the Raptors would stand a chance of drawing out the series. If nothing else, another name was thrown in the hat with which Nurse could contemplate big time lineup changes. He'd get a single day to sort out his plan. Toronto would be playing to save its season in Game 3 back at home. ∎

Raptors 118, Bucks 112 (2OT)
May 19, 2019 • Toronto, Ontario

WINNING THE MARATHON

Leonard and the Raptors Outlast the Bucks, Get Back into Series

By Sean Woodley

Superstars thrust teams into the realm of contention. But more often than not, it's out-of-body experiences by role players that win championship rings. Toronto got the best of both in Game 3 of the Eastern Conference Finals.

The Raptors' first game back home since Kawhi Leonard ended the Sixers was as close to do-or-die that it gets. No team in history has ever clawed out of a 3-0 hole in a best-of-seven series. To make up that ground against this Bucks team was beyond realism.

Nick Nurse faced something of a crossroads in the lead-up to the game. His choices: stick with the same starting lineup that had dominated opponents all spring but faltered two games straight, or toss the Scrabble pieces back in the bag and start shaking. Danny Green's shooting slump was weeks old by that point; Marc Gasol looked every one of his 34 years old over two games in Milwaukee. At the very least, Nurse could have justified a straight Green-for-Norman Powell swap. He even tossed around the phrase "lineup changes" at his media availabilities between games.

In a move that highlighted the difference between Nurse and his more panicky predecessor Dwane Casey, Toronto's head coach stuck with what got his team to the Conference Finals in the first place. Powell saw an uptick in minutes, and the defensive assignments of the starters were mixed around. Otherwise? Stasis.

"Well, I said lineup changes; I didn't say starting lineup changes," Nurse said cheekily when pressed about his decisions after the game. "We played a lot of different lineups tonight, and we changed at least three if not four of the matchups to start the game. And then we brought Norm in early and Serge (Ibaka) in early, and we went big. So, I think some of those things, some of those changes, were pretty good to us."

Those small tweaks included a dropping of the hammer. Kawhi Leonard, one of the best perimeter defenders of the last 20 years — if not of all-time — would slide over to be Giannis Antetokounmpo's primary defender. It was a choice that changed the tenor of the series.

Nurse's changes (or lack thereof) helped Toronto leap out to a 30-21 lead to end the first. Powell subbed in for Green around the halfway point and poured in a third of Toronto's points on 80 percent shooting. Gasol made good on Nurse's belief. As the hub of the Raptors' offense, the Spaniard finished his first 10-minute stint with eight points, three rebounds, and four assists. His contributions weren't relegated to the low-stakes opening moments of Game 3, though.

Much like the way Game 1's script unfolded, Toronto found itself warding off the Bucks to lesser degrees of success as the night wore on. Milwaukee's defense tightened, yielding 19 points in each of the middle quarters as the Bucks inched closer and closer to par. George Hill — a Raptors tormentor of postseasons past

Kawhi Leonard was terrific in the huge Game 3 win with 36 points, nine rebounds, and five assists.

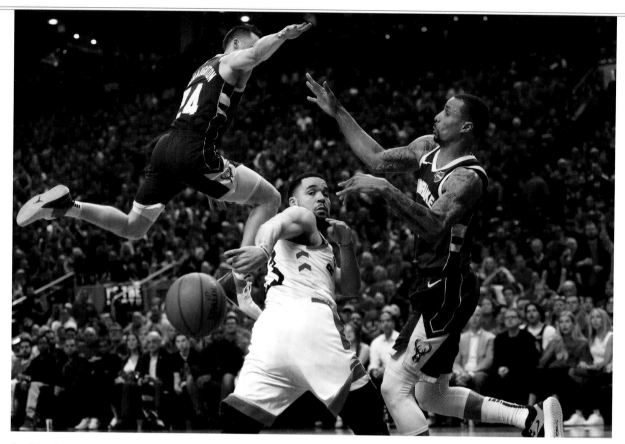

Fred VanVleet continued to struggle with his shot, going 1-of-11 from the floor, but did dish out six assists in the win.

— ripped off a 7-of-9 shooting performance to lead his team with 24 points off the bench. Malcolm Brogdon provided 20 more from the reserve crew, showcasing the distinct, on-paper edge the Bucks held over the Raptors in the department of guard depth. Fred VanVleet had made just six shots since the end of the first round. Green was losing time to Powell, who'd been benched as recently as Game 7 against Philly. Through 36 minutes the pair had missed all 10 of their combined attempts from the floor. Milwaukee trimmed the Raps' lead to just two heading into a fourth quarter upon which the entire season would hinge.

As has been standard in Raptors games since his arrival in The North back in 2012, Kyle Lowry was the engine powering most of Toronto's success in Game 3. He'd been navigating foul trouble — a common side effect of his balls-to-the-wall playing style. Still, his 11 points, four rebounds, and five assists were a calming force for the Raptors under the most intense of circumstances. Fluidity was restored to the offense any time he'd check back in. His necessity was why Nick Nurse rolled the dice by subbing Lowry in with 7:11 to

play, disqualification just a single foul away. The Raptors led by just three at the time. Lowry was essential to a game-winning push.

His first order of business was setting up a Powell three to double the lead. But then, a couple possessions later, disaster: a loose-ball battle, a whistle blast from official Ed Malloy, and a sixth foul for Lowry. With 6:12 to play and the chilly VanVleet checking in to run the team, Toronto's six-point cushion almost felt like a deficit. Blood was in the water. Kawhi Leonard's solo stardom was not going to be enough to hold off the frenzied Bucks. If a Raptors supporting piece had one of those run-sustaining outbursts to offer up, now was the time.

It so happened that Leonard had a couple guys around him pop when they were needed most.

Gasol, playing with five fouls from the 5:11 mark on, was masterful on both ends, clearing the glass, playmaking in lieu of the departed Lowry, and orchestrating the defense that bent but didn't break down the stretch.

"He's a pro. He's a great player," said Mike Budenholzer of Gasol at the post-game podium. "I'm sure him taking responsibility ... it just speaks to his

Marc Gasol (left) battles for the ball with Khris Middleton. Gasol was indispensable in the double-overtime win with 16 points, 12 rebounds, seven assists, and five blocks.

character and he came out and had a great game tonight."

VanVleet helped keep Toronto afloat, too. His first and only make of the night came from long range with 3:18 on the clock. His work as a help defender, aiding the foul-troubled Gasol around the rim, was vital.

Their efforts set the stage for Pascal Siakam to seal the win with a pair of free throws, up 96-94, with seven seconds left to tick. Under the heft of the moment, Siakam missed both. On Milwaukee's next inbound, Khris Middleton drove and got blocked by VanVleet at the rim, only to recover the miss and put it back. Overtime.

The next five minutes were engine sludge incarnate. Neither defense budged for a minute and a half, when Green, in for a fouled-out Powell, turned his 0-of-8 night into 1-of-9. With just a 7-7 score line through 4:46 of OT, Leonard had an opportunity to end a second straight game at Scotiabank Arena with a buzzer-beater. This time his mid-range jumper failed to blow the roof off the joint. Double overtime.

Early in the second overtime, Antetokounmpo joined the six-foul brigade, leaving Leonard as the lone superstar left on the court. What followed was a four-minute mixtape of reasons why the Raptors swung the deal for Leonard. He finished off the Bucks with a surge of eight points, a steal, and a rebound. On the back of 36-9-5 in a career-high 52 minutes from their superhuman small forward, Toronto pulled out the 118-112 win.

"It's amazing. What he's been doing for us all year, especially in the postseason," Powell exclaimed after the win. "He's a guy that all he wants to do is win. He doesn't care about the accolades, the points. As long as he's out there helping the team win, that's good for us. We feed off of that. He's a great leader for us. To be able to go out there and play 52 minutes and lead the team with his voice in the timeouts, telling us to stay calm, stay in the moment, not get anxious — it's amazing to have a guy like that on the team."

Toronto had a challenging road ahead. Milwaukee had only lost back-to-back games once during its historic regular season. The Raptors were wiped; the younger Bucks still favored to advance despite dropping such an emotionally-charged game. But the Raptors had "a guy like that" on their side. Because of that fact alone, there was a chance. ∎

Raptors 120, Bucks 102
May 21, 2019 • Toronto, Ontario

BREATHING ROOM

Toronto Gets Much-Needed Easy Win, Evens the Series at Two

By Sean Woodley

Complete team efforts were hard to come by for the Raptors through 15 games in the playoffs. Kawhi Leonard had done so much to pace the team on a nightly basis; Pascal Siakam and Kyle Lowry usually joined in the fun. Night to night, who filled the remaining gaps was anyone's guess. If no one brought the glue, the Raptors were likely to lose.

So, it was refreshing to see the Raptors, on a night where Leonard began to show signs of all the miles he'd logged as Toronto's playoff horse, bring it from top-to-bottom. With contributions from all angles, the Raptors made what should have been their most difficult win of the playoffs yet look like a cinch.

Serge Ibaka warned his teammates of the challenge that loomed in the effort to even the series at twos. He'd been in the Raptors' East Finals predicament before. Back in 2012, Ibaka was a core member of the Oklahoma City Thunder squad that stomped out the Spurs (featuring Danny Green and a rookie version of Leonard) in four-straight after an 0-2 start.

It makes sense, then, that Ibaka helped spark the Raptors to pull away in the second quarter of Game 4 after a threatening Milwaukee start. Of Ibaka's 17 points and 13 rebounds over the course of a high-energy performance, 10 and seven came during a single eight-minute stretch of work in the second. Toronto won the quarter by nine and never looked back.

Mercifully, finally, all three of Toronto's rotation reserves played well in concert. Powell reached heat-check mode by the end of the third quarter with the game out of reach. While his 18 points on 18 shots weren't the height of efficient basketball, the mere fact that someone not named Leonard led the team in attempts was a welcome deviation from the rote plot points Toronto had adhered to all spring. Fred VanVleet's out-of-control death spiral of a slump halted for good, too. The dam exploded open in the form of a 5-of-6 shooting line and a perfect stroke on three triples — all just hours removed from the birth of his second child, Fred Jr., the apparent source of his rediscovered powers.

Asked if Game 4 was the most complete performance by the Raptors as a team through the playoffs, Ibaka offered:

"I think so. This playoff so far, yes. We need it from — our team need it from us, you know, coming off the bench to bring some energy and defensive intensity and score some points to help our starting lineup. I think it was big time for us tonight."

The starters were great, too. Marc Gasol managed his second consecutive "best game as a Raptor." Siakam's

Kyle Lowry raises up for the shot with Bucks centre Brook Lopez challenging. Lowry was the star of the game for Toronto, scoring 25 points, grabbing five rebounds, and dishing out six assists.

quiet seven points were complemented by six assists. Kyle Lowry poured in 25 points on just 11 attempts from the floor and a parade to the free-throw line and was the best player on the floor from start-to-finish.

Leonard got a reprieve from the burden of his greatness for at least one night — one that turned out to be perfectly timed. Coming off the marathon of Game 3, Leonard looked to be bothered by a lingering leg issue. After a monstrous, and-1 cram in the face of Antetokounmpo in the third quarter, Leonard gingerly walked to take his spot at the free throw line. He didn't quite look right for the rest of the evening. Between his diminished burst and the Bucks' commitment to smothering him with bodies and limbs any time he ventured near the paint, the supporting cast picked a good time to start knocking down open shots. Leonard's single accredited assist belied the job he did in shepherding Toronto's offense along. Hockey assists were his currency in Game 4. Garbage time in the fourth helped limit Leonard to a manageable 34 minutes.

With the Raptors finally congealing into a team of eight connected guys, and the series now even after an 18-point drubbing, it was the Bucks who had been pushed to the back foot (or hoof?). Mike Budenholzer would face some questions ahead of Game 5 back in Milwaukee. How he answered them would likely determine the Eastern Conference champions. ■

Kawhi Leonard dunks with authority as Giannis Antetokounmpo defends. Leonard had 19 points in the comfortable Game 4 win.

Raptors 105, Bucks 99
May 23, 2019 • Milwaukee, Wisconsin

ROAD TESTED

Toronto Gets First Win By Either Team on the Road, Sets Up Clinching Game 6

By Sean Woodley

Of all the clichés that get tossed around at playoff time, the idea that a series doesn't begin in earnest until a home team loses is among the ones that rings the truest. The later said home loss takes place, the direr the straights for the team that yields it.

Going into Game 5 back in Milwaukee, the smart money was on the Bucks to win. Three-straight Ls could not be found on their 2018-19 game log, playoffs or regular season. Throw in the madness of Fiserv Forum as a road environment to try and steal a game from, and the Raptors were in a tough spot. After dropping the two first games of the series, the realistic best-case scenario was to swap home wins and try to steal a Game 7 back on the road.

Early in Game 5 it seemed as though that would be the only route forward for Toronto. Eric Bledsoe, invisible for much of the series, was at his marauding, tempo-driving best during an 18-4 Bucks run to open the game. An outcome similar to the Bucks' wire-to-wire jog in Game 2 seemed afoot.

One of the central questions about the 2018-19 Raptors was one of identity. With all of the player turnover and varied skills on either side of the ball, it was an impossible team to pin down. However, if one through line of the postseason could be used to sum up this version of the Raptors, it was probably the team's unflinchingly strong chin. These Raptors could take a punch.

Toronto replied to Milwaukee's haymaker not with a heavy counterstrike, but rather a sound defensive pose. After getting blitzed for 32 first quarter points, the Raptors settled into the kind of terrifying defensive groove they'd used to smother opponents and steal games all season. It was a vicious, inescapable cycle — defensive stand, rebound, fast break, bucket, lather, rinse, repeat.

"We want to be a good defensive team," said Leonard after Game 5. "That's what we look at in film and everybody comments or has something to say that's knowledgeable to try to make our defense better, and we go into the game and try to execute it as best we can."

Another stretch of maniacal defense became a necessity in the third quarter as another Bucks push threatened to thrust Milwaukee ahead for good.

Giannis Antetokounmpo's dunks have a demoralizing quality to them. You can do everything right to wall his seven-foot frame off from the paint, and oftentimes he'll still find a way to cram it simply because he's faster, longer, and more explosive than you. If you're lucky he'll refrain from yelling in your face afterwards. One of those potentially back-breaking dunks put the Bucks up 63-51 with 7:43 to play in the third quarter. A team with a lesser chin may have packed it in

Pascal Siakam finishes in transition with Malcolm Brogdon (13) and Giannis Antetokounmpo (34) looking on. Siakam had 14 points and 13 rebounds in the road win.

then and there. Instead, the Raptors conjured another defensive tidal wave, accompanied by a deadly, Leonard-orchestrated offensive attack.

Mike Budenholzer had come under some scrutiny after Game 4 for his defensive approach. Selling out to stop Leonard with multiple defenders left Milwaukee prone to wide open looks from role players. Toronto's off-ball shooters were almost exclusively good-to-very good from long range. It was a dangerous recipe for the Bucks.

Of course, these are the quandaries a player like Leonard imposed upon every defense he steamrolled through on the road to the NBA title. Defending him perfectly is nearly impossible — particularly when his playmaking is at the level it was in Game 5.

Leonard set a playoff career-high with nine assists, every last one of them coming on a Raptors three-pointer. All told he either scored or set up 62 of Toronto's 105 points. Eventually, he softened up Milwaukee's defense enough to take it to the Bucks on his own.

"They were sending two or three bodies at him and kind of tilting the floor and making sure guys were loaded on him," said Lowry of Leonard's offensive progression throughout the evening. "He was making the right passes, and we made some shots for him tonight. And then third quarter, he just — he's been doing it all playoffs … The game he played tonight, 35, 9, and 7 was a pretty good game. It's a pretty good game on the big stage and on the road. Superstar. Superstar."

The superstar dropped 15 of his 35 points in the fourth quarter. More malicious than any of his other buckets were the back-to-back threes he drained over the top of Brook Lopez to take the Raptors from down two to up four inside a minute. Toronto never trailed again in Game 5.

With a 3-2 lead in hand, they'd return to Toronto for a chance to advance to the first NBA Finals in franchise history. Just as unprecedented as the achievement the Raptors were on the precipice of unlocking was the scene waiting for them back in Toronto that Saturday night. ■

The Raptors swarm Bucks point guard Eric Bledsoe as he gets up a shot in the lane. Toronto limited Milwaukee's high-powered offense to just 99 points in the win.

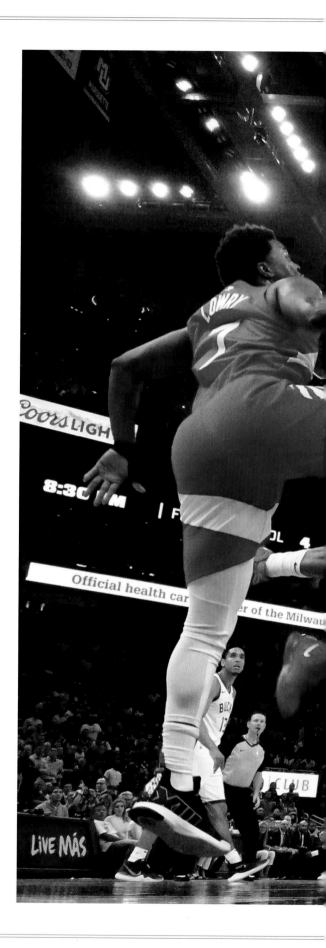

Raptors 100, Bucks 94
May 25, 2019 • Toronto, Ontario

KINGS OF THE EAST!

Raptors Clinch Berth to NBA Finals with Four-Straight Wins

By Sean Woodley

The area occupying the tail end of Toronto's Bremner Boulevard, hemmed in by York Street to the west, Union Station to the North, and Scotiabank Arena (née Air Canada Centre) to the East used to just be called Maple Leaf Square. Equipped with an enormous screen on the exterior wall of the arena, typically used to advertise upcoming concerts and shows, the area always had the potential to be a public meeting ground.

It was Toronto Maple Leafs fans who first took advantage of the square. In 2013, the Leafs made their first playoff appearance in nine years. The city's toughest ticket was also its most expensive. So priced-out fans gathered outside to huddle together through whatever vile weather late-April in Toronto could muster to watch their team. That particular series went poorly. Boston eliminated the Leafs in Game 7, coming back from down 4-1 with under 10 minutes to play to win 5-4 in overtime. The loss emptied the square for another year. But a city-wide tradition was born.

Over the next few years, as the Leafs dipped back into irrelevance and the Lowry-DeRozan-Casey Raptors hit the upswing of their win curve, it was Raptors fans who flocked to the patch of concrete just outside the arena walls. In a colloquial evolution mirroring the city's ever-growing addition to hoops, Maple Leaf Square

became known by a more recognizable name: Jurassic Park. During its first day of operation in 2014 ahead of Game 1 against the Nets, Masai Ujiri famously screamed "[Bleep] Brooklyn!" before dropping the mic in front of a sea of fans, setting the tone early for the ferocity fans in the square would exude in those early days of Toronto's half decade-long run to the title.

Toronto's commitment to the bit wasn't always steadfast. Much like it was with the Maple Leafs, Jurassic Park became the place where fans who could no longer afford the exorbitant prices to sit inside would go to experience the next closest thing. As the Raptors' playoff disappointments piled up, folks became a little less gung-ho to stand around when the weather was rotten. Crowds for away games became reliably sparse.

But not during this playoff run. Not with Kawhi Leonard ushering in a new sense of belief in the team's odds of not falling flat. And certainly not with a berth in the Finals on the line.

Game 6 of the Eastern Conference Finals didn't tip off until 8:30pm on Saturday the 25th. Five hours before tip — three hours before the gates to Jurassic Park opened — the line to get in was wrapped around a city block. Nearly a kilometer's worth of people, standing in line for the right to stand. With passage to the first Finals in team history a possibility, folks understandably wanted to be as

Kawhi Leonard dunks over Giannis Antetokounmpo in the second half of the historic Game 6 win. Leonard had 27 points, 17 rebounds, and seven assists in the clinching victory.

close as possible to the epicentre of the coming earthquake. They would not be left disappointed, although for a time it seemed like they would.

Giannis Antetokounmpo promised before Game 1 that the Bucks were not going to go the way of Bambi's mum.

"We're not gonna fold," Antetokounmpo asserted after the home loss in Game 5. "We're the best team in the league. We're gonna go in, give it everything we got. We can't fold."

The Bucks lived up to their best player's vow.

Milwaukee's half-court defense constricted the life out of Toronto's attack early on. A 31-18 lead after one was built on diligence on defense, and stream of fire shooting from the team's fingertips on offense. Six of the nine threes Milwaukee fired up in the quarter found bottom. Nearly two full quarters of failed attempts to chase down and lasso the Bucks later, the Raptors found themselves trailing 76-61 with just 14:18 of game time remaining. Scoring 15 points, period, in that allotment of time was an odious ask considering the fervour with which the Bucks defended to that point.

But as had been the case throughout run its through the East, Toronto's defense was no slouch, either. The 2019 Raptors perpetually occupied a space wherein they were a four-minute defensive deluge from snatching control of a game. With 2:18 to play in the third and Antetokounmpo subbing out for scheduled rest, it was high time they put together one of those stretches.

Kawhi Leonard took it upon himself to ignite Toronto's last gasp. His stretch of play in the final two-plus minutes of the third will go down as perhaps the greatest ever blip of dominance by a Raptor, and certainly the timeliest. Toronto ended the quarter on a 10-0 run to cut the lead from 15 to five, entirely thanks to Leonard's doing.

First, he muscled his way to three-point play. A quick mid-range jumper followed. Next, he picked out

Kyle Lowry attacks the basket while George Hill (right) attempts to bother the shot. Lowry had 17 points and eight assists in the win.

Serge Ibaka for an easy finish under the basket. And lastly, a sequence of determination that only postseason desperation can give rise to: after picking up a three-shot foul and missing the third look from the line, Leonard lunged after his own brick, collecting it with his vacuum palms, and earning another trip to the line on a Bucks loose-ball foul. He hit both gimmes and Toronto trailed by five, but the look in Leonard's eyes suggested no Bucks lead would last long in the fourth quarter.

As it turned out, the Raptors didn't even need Leonard on the floor to continue the onslaught he provoked. With Kyle Lowry conducting as per usual, a bench-heavy lineup poured it on to open what would end up being the final quarter of Milwaukee's season. A single Brook Lopez bucket was the only moment in which Toronto's defense relented in the opening four minutes of the quarter; Leonard was able to steal rest for three and a half of those. After he subbed back in, a Fred VanVleet three — his 14th in 17 tries since the start of Game 4 — and an Ibaka hook shot opened the Raptors' lead up to six.

A couple possessions later, Lowry poked the ball out of the grasp of Khris Middleton and raced down the floor with the stolen goods. Leveling his behind into Antetokounmpo, he cleared the runway for an exclamation point. With a dump off to Leonard, and a soaring lefty dunk into the body of The Greek Freak, Toronto's other-worldly megastar shot the Scotiabank Arena roof into the ozone layer. Toronto led 87-79. The scent of the Finals began wafting through the concourse.

Full credit belongs to Milwaukee for their response. Out of the Leonard-induced timeout called by Budenholzer, the Bucks quickly pulled to within one. A Game 7 was still on the table, but not really. As a Leonard three-pointer from the right corner rattled off rim, then backboard, and through the mesh to put Toronto up 95-90, even Milwaukee must have been resigned to the

charmed nature of this Raptors run. The east end rim at Scotiabank Arena should be sent to the Hall of Fame after its work in the 2019 playoffs.

A series of reviews and timeouts delayed the official start of the celebrations. Toronto's fans had waited patiently for 24 years to see their team in the NBA Finals. What was a few more seconds?

With a George Hill miss and the sounding of the final buzzer, elation enveloped a team, an arena, and a city. You could have killed the arena lights and Kyle Lowry's smile would have done their job. All of the heartbreak of previous playoff exits, the sour feelings in the wake of the DeMar DeRozan-for-Leonard trade, and the questions over whether the deal was worth the gamble evaporated to form the haze that shrouded the city in glee for days. A trip to the Finals had been booked. Game 1 would take place in Toronto on Thursday night. And as Masai Ujiri shouted to the beautiful lunatics in the crowd as the Eastern Conference championship trophy was presented, the Raptors were not satisfied.

"We came all this way to compete and we want to win in Toronto — and we will in in Toronto," Ujiri emoted on the mic in front of the crowd, the way he did all the way back in 2014 during the opening of Jurassic Park, just with fewer profanities. ∎

The longest-tenured member of the Raptors, Lowry celebrates clinching the Eastern Conference championship with his family.